ORTHO'S All About

Additions

Meredith® Books
Des Moines, Iowa

Ortho® Books
An imprint of Meredith® Books

Ortho's All About Additions
Editor: Larry Johnston
Contributing Writer: Charlie Wing
Art Director: Tom Wegner
Assistant Art Director: Harijs Priekulis
Copy Chief: Catherine Hamrick
Copy and Production Editor: Terri Fredrickson
Book Production Managers: Pam Kvitne,
    Marjorie J. Schenkelberg
Contributing Copy Editor: Steve Hallam
Technical Proofreader: Ray Kast
Contributing Proofreaders: Dan Degen, David Krause,
    Debra Morris Smith, JoEllyn Wittke
Indexer: Barbara L. Klein
Editorial and Design Assistants: Renee E. McAtee,
    Karen McFadden
Edit and Design Production Coordinator: Mary Lee Gavin

Additional Editorial Contributions from
    Art Rep Services
Director: Chip Nadeau
Designer: lk Design
Illustrator: Dave Brandon

Meredith® Books
Editor in Chief: Linda Raglan Cunningham
Design Director: Matt Strelecki
Managing Editor: Gregory H. Kayko
Executive Editor: Benjamin W. Allen

Publisher: James D. Blume
Executive Director, Marketing: Jeffrey Myers
Executive Director, New Business Development:
    Todd M. Davis
Executive Director, Sales: Ken Zagor
Director, Operations: George A. Susral
Director, Production: Douglas M. Johnston
Business Director: Jim Leonard

Vice President and General Manager: Douglas J. Guendel

Meredith Publishing Group
President, Publishing Group: Stephen M. Lacy
Vice President-Publishing Director: Bob Mate

Meredith Corporation
Chairman and Chief Executive Officer: William T. Kerr

In Memoriam: E.T. Meredith III (1933-2003)

Thanks to
Colleen Johnson

Photographers
    (Photographers credited may retain copyright ©
    to their photographs.)
D. Randolph Foulds
Rick Taylor

Cover photo: Jeffrey Rycus

All of us at Ortho® Books are dedicated to providing you
with the information and ideas you need to enhance your
home and garden. We welcome your comments and
suggestions about this book. Write to us at:
    Meredith Corporation
    Ortho Books
    1716 Locust St.
    Des Moines, IA 50309–3023

If you would like more information on other Ortho
products, call 800-225-2883 or visit us at www.ortho.com

Note to the Readers: Due to differing conditions, tools,
and individual skills, Meredith Corporation assumes no
responsibility for any damages, injuries suffered, or losses
incurred as a result of following the information published
in this book. Before beginning any project, review the
instructions carefully, and if any doubts or questions remain,
consult local experts or authorities. Because codes and
regulations vary greatly, you always should check with
authorities to ensure that your project complies with all
applicable local codes and regulations. Always read and
observe all of the safety precautions provided by
manufacturers of any tools, equipment, or supplies,
and follow all accepted safety procedures.

GETTING STARTED   4

FOUNDATIONS   24

BUILDING THE SHELL   40

THE FINAL DETAILS   64

KITCHENS AND BATHS   94

INDEX   110

METRIC CONVERSIONS   112

GETTING STARTED

When your growing family, more affluent lifestyle, or at-home business no longer fits comfortably into your home, you have to take action. Your choices are to reorganize wasted space in your home, buy or build a larger home, or add on to your existing home.

WHEN ADDING ON MAKES SENSE

Adding on is worth considering if you like your home and neighborhood, you have a mature landscape, or you don't want to give up cherished memories.

Saving money is not a primary reason to add on. Building an addition will cost as much per square foot as building a new home. It may also require some remodeling of your home to allow the new and old spaces to work harmoniously. To keep an addition from looking clumsy or tacked-on, it should blend with the style of your existing home, so you might need to hire an architect or designer. And additional electrical, heating, and cooling loads might require upgrading of those systems.

Whether you build the addition yourself, manage the job while others do the work, or hand it all to a general contractor, you can make better decisions if you understand what goes into a project of such scope. This book describes the steps in building an addition, from laying out the foundation to installing interior moldings—everything you need to know to succeed in adding on to your house.

The best additions blend with the home's original architecture. This new family room right uses the same cladding material—painted brick—and features the same roof slope as does the main house, helping to make the addition look as though it might have been there all along. Plantings and a patio also help blend the new with the old.

The master suite left uses vertical windows that complement the home's original fenestration.

IS AN ADDITION FOR YOU?

Kitchens—always the busiest of rooms—are popular additions, as they can often benefit from more space.

An addition can provide the extra space you need without the disruption of a move. Before the hammers start swinging, however, make sure your project will meet your family's present and future needs by answering these questions:

■ What kind of house do you need? Is your present home's arrangement close enough to what you want that adding on a room or two will give you all the space you need? Or do you need so many changes that building new makes more sense?

■ Can your present house accept an addition? Not all homes are worth adding on to. The inadequacies of an older home can be magnified by the new materials used in an addition. Existing aspects that seemed passable, such as the roof, siding, and windows, may suddenly look worn and tired. Systems serving the house, such as electrical, heating, and plumbing, may not support an addition, requiring modification or replacement. Zoning regulations, utility easements, and setback requirements may

make the addition you envision difficult or impossible to achieve. Get the whole picture before you start your project, and decide whether the addition you want is practical.

■ What makes the most sense in terms of investment? Is it wiser to invest $20,000 or $30,000 in your present home or to sell the house and invest the equity in a new home? That depends on your situation. If you have a small house in a neighborhood of mansions, updating may substantially increase its worth. On the flip side, a $300,000 house sitting in a $200,000 neighborhood may reduce the likelihood of any return on your investment. If you plan to sell your house within a few years, consider saving your improvements for your next home. If you plan to live in a home for the rest of your life, let your heart, not just your investment portfolio, decide which is the best option for you.

An addition can be a great way to add modern amenities such as large windows, vaulted ceilings, and big gathering spaces to vintage homes, which often lack such luxuries.

Master suites are increasingly common in new homes and are often added to older homes. They're good candidates for an addition, as it is often desirable to set them apart from the rest of the house.

BUMPING OUT

Now that you've decided an addition is what you need, the question becomes: What kind?

The least disruptive—and least expensive—is often a bump-out. From adding a small seating alcove or convenient breakfast nook to pushing out a wall, bump-outs can be a great way to add space where you need it most, without breaking the bank or tearing up the whole house. These mini-additions are typically up to 4 feet deep and range from a few feet wide to the full length of a wall. A bump-out is less expensive to build than a full-blown addition because the new space "hangs" on an exterior wall and does not require a new foundation.

Although the square-footage gain is generally small, the effect of a bump-out can be great—especially if windows or skylights illuminate a previously dim room or pull in distant views.

This small bump-out adds a cozy space to tuck an inviting whirlpool tub into this master suite. The new space looks as if were always a part of this bathroom.

The bump-out looks just as authentic from the outside; it's finished in an appropriate style to match the home's Tudor architecture. The bump-out's roof supports a third-story balcony off the master bedroom, adding two spaces for the price of one.

BUMP-OUT DOS AND DON'TS

■ Do check setback requirements with your planning and zoning commission. If you don't have sufficient room to build a bump-out, you may be able to get a zoning variance. Prepare for your local zoning meeting; bring accurate information, such as the distance between your house and the property line.

■ Do insulate well. You're adding space that needs to be heated and cooled by your existing climate-control system. Make that job easier by insulating your new space well. If you're adding lots of glass, consider specifying energy-saving double- or triple-pane windows, low-E coatings, and insulating shades.

■ Don't necessarily copy the cladding materials of your original house. Such a match may be difficult, expensive, or impossible. If the original cladding materials are no longer available, look for compatible materials rather than those that match exactly.

■ Do blend the colors of the bump-out with the house. If you decide to use matching materials, you may have to paint the original house, as paint colors fade over time.

BUMPING OUT
continued

A towering back-of-the-house bump-out adds about 70 square feet on each level of this bungalow. The addition seems much bigger: Lots of glass and a spacious deck bring in the wide-open outdoors— without eating up precious yard space on this tight, urban lot.

LIVING WITHIN THE LAW

Before you start planning your addition, meet at least briefly with your local building code officials to see if you need a building permit to do what you're hoping to do, and to make sure your project won't violate any zoning restrictions.

On the main living level, the bumpout creates a sunny landing area surrounded by decking. At the top of the stairs, it provides a screened-in porch. Because the addition is in the back of the house and flanked by tall trees, it blends well with its surroundings.

SPEC YOUR STORAGE!

Plan for built-ins and storage. If you're bumping out and adding a window seat, include drawers or a chest-like storage area beneath to catch such things as children's toys or guest-room linens. If you're adding a whole room, build enough storage space to hold everything you'll need in the room you're creating—and perhaps some extra, such as built-in shelves for display.

BUMPING UP

Nestled among ranch houses, this well-done bump-up may start a trend. Its roofline and siding materials keep the style and scale in sync with its neighbors.

If you need more space than a simple bump-out can provide, but still don't want the expense of digging a new foundation, your best solution may be to raise the roof.

From adding a top-floor master retreat to doubling the size of your existing house—without disturbing the yard—a bump-up can allow you to make dramatic changes without changing your address. It's a particularly good solution when a small yard or city zoning restrictions force you to go up, not out, when you need more space.

There are other advantages to going over the top when you add on: It's generally less expensive than adding a similarly sized wing to your home. And you can often tie in electrical and plumbing to existing systems with a minimum of additional runs. Bump-ups can also be a way to take advantage of a view.

Here's another ranch that grew—without overwhelming its neighbors. To keep costs down, the house's original footprint and first-floor room arrangements were retained, as were several architectural elements, such as the centered entryway and bay window. Topping the original entry with a study creates a new exterior focal point; residing the entire house in white shingles unifies the addition with the original structure.

Prior to the addition of a second floor (shown above), this home looked like tens of thousands of suburban tract houses built in the 1950s and 1960s. Its transformation just goes to show the magic that a well-conceived addition can work.

BUMPING UP
continued

SECOND STORY

Before you add another story to your home:

■ **GET A PRO'S ADVICE.** An architect or structural engineer can tell you whether your house can support the weight of a second story.

■ **BE PREPARED FOR EXTRA WORK.** Your existing walls and footings may need to be reinforced, adding to costs.

■ **CONSIDER THE WEATHER.** Removing and replacing your roof is not something you want to do during the rainy season. Plan carefully to ensure that this stage is completed quickly.

This formerly squat lakeside cottage was topped with a second story, a budget-savvy way to double the size of the house. A dramatic, bumped-out entryway and attached pergola create a grand entrance.

Before.

This cottage is situated on a lake, and the second-story sitting area commands a sweeping vista that a lower-level addition couldn't match.

BUILDING ON

You can add anything from a new room to a whole new wing to your house by building on to the side, back, or even the front.

If you have the space, this type of remodeling works well for a home office or studio, a master suite, a mudroom or utility room, or a guest apartment. All of these can benefit from some separation from the core of the original house. The scale of the work can be considerable, though: digging and pouring a new foundation, upgrading mechanicals to handle the new space, and landscaping considerations can make large build-on projects almost as complicated as building a whole house.

This addition turns a linear house into an L-shape design, adding interest to the exterior. A welcoming porch surrounds the new wing. Matching roof pitches, window styles, trim details, and siding help the new blend seamlessly with the old. Inside, a new master suite fills the addition's second floor, and a family room adds flexibility to the main level.

When building on, it's often helpful to work with your total design team to develop a site plan, to integrate landscape design with the home's new footprint. This project took advantage of the addition's sheltering wall to create a cozy courtyard.

BUILDING ON
continued

Whether you call it a sunroom, conservatory, or solarium, a glass-enclosed room has an exotic allure, letting you bask in sunshine without ever leaving home. It's also a great way to open up your house to the surrounding yard, gardens, or vista without making changes to original rooms. This sunroom, added to the back of an older home, has walls of windows and a roof of glass that place occupants almost in the middle of a garden. Climbing roses and other flowers envelop the addition.

Inside, casual wicker furniture and a sunken hot tub invite lingering. Potted plants surround the tub, further merging the room with the garden.

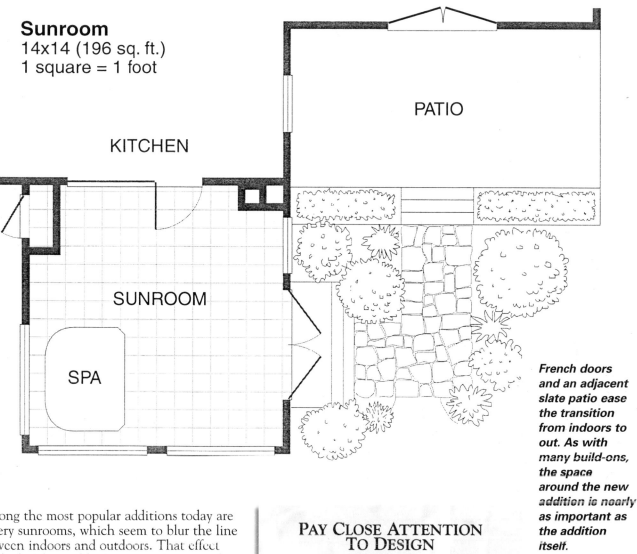

Sunroom
14x14 (196 sq. ft.)
1 square = 1 foot

KITCHEN

PATIO

SUNROOM

SPA

French doors and an adjacent slate patio ease the transition from indoors to out. As with many build-ons, the space around the new addition is nearly as important as the addition itself.

Among the most popular additions today are cheery sunrooms, which seem to blur the line between indoors and outdoors. That effect can be heightened by incorporating potted plants, casual furnishings, tile flooring, and water features such as hot tubs or fountains.

Sunrooms can bring new vitality to older houses that feel restricted by small rooms and narrow, paned windows. In the home shown opposite, for example, the new sunroom has become a favorite spot in which its owners can relax. "The sunroom with the hot tub is the best thing we ever did," one says.

If you're interested in adding a sunroom, you have a couple options. You can add a greenhouse wall to the south side of your home, creating additional living space while providing an ideal place to grow plants. Some greenhouse additions can even help heat your home with passive solar energy. Others are available in kit form, reducing the cost while providing several size, type, and style options.

Or, you can go all-out with a custom-designed solarium addition such as this one. Either way, it's a great way to bring the outdoors in.

PAY CLOSE ATTENTION TO DESIGN

Because building on represents a significant change in the original home's footprint, you may want to hire an architect to ensure that the addition doesn't detract from the appeal—and thus the value—of the original house. You'll also want to make sure that the new space is thoughtfully integrated with the old, so traffic flows as well or better after the addition as it did before.

Building on can have a great impact on your yard as well as your home, so consider its placement and orientation carefully. Discuss with your addition's designer any trees or other landscape features that you'd like to leave undisturbed. Consider designing the addition to create a courtyard or patio, thus adding outdoor living space as well as shelter. Discuss any reworking of planting and other yard features, and take these into account when budgeting the project.

HIRING HELP

Hiring an architect isn't necessarily inexpensive, but they can often recoup their fee with clever design and careful materials selections.

Association of Home Builders Remodelers Council (NAHB) (800/368-5242 Ext. 8216; www.nahb.com).

EXPLORE. Call the architects and contractors on your list—you should have at least four from each profession—and ask for references. Then contact the people they name and ask them to recount their positive and negative experiences. Also, if you see a recent remodeling project that you like, contact the homeowners and ask about their experience and results.

EVALUATE. Based on these references, interview the top three professionals who make the cut and tour some of their finished projects. Experienced architects and contractors will ask you questions as well to find out your expectations and needs. You should come away from each interview and tour with an idea of the quality of their work and how well your personalities and visions for the project jibe.

USE THESE TACTICS TO TRACK DOWN THE BEST ONE FOR YOU

GATHER. Collect names of professionals to investigate and interview. Ask friends and colleagues for suggestions and recommendations. Identify local referrals with the help of professional organizations, such as the American Institute of Architects (AIA) (800/242-3837; www.aia.org), or the National

SOLICIT PRELIMINARY DRAWINGS AND BIDS. To narrow your decision between two or more architects, it may be worth the additional cost to solicit preliminary drawings from each one. This is a great way to test your working relationship. In the same vein, ask contractors for bids. Don't base your decision on cost alone. Instead, weigh what you learned in the interview with the thoroughness of the bid itself.

REMODELING SURVIVAL TIPS

When your home transforms into a construction zone, the mess can make you wonder if your life will ever be back to normal. To ensure the minor inconveniences of a remodeling project don't become major headaches, discuss cleanup with your contractor before work begins. Ask for an overview of the entire construction process. Together, develop a plan to minimize disruption.

DISCUSS WHAT THE CONTRACTOR WILL DO TO CONTROL DUST. Most contractors tape a plastic barrier at doorways to reduce dust from the construction zone. Some may also tape off heat registers and change the furnace filters daily, especially when sanding drywall.

REQUEST FLOOR PROTECTION. Specify that walkways and carpeted areas that lead to the construction zone be

covered with drop cloths or plastic runners.

REALIZE THAT NOISE IS INEVITABLE. Ask workers to arrive and leave at reasonable hours. Understand that if you set shorter work days, you may lengthen, the duration of the project.

COORDINATE SCHEDULES. Let the contractor know in advance if there are any times, such as holidays or special family events, when your house will be off-limits.

SET UP SOME "TEMPORARY ROOMS." If you're remodeling the kitchen, for example, move the refrigerator, the coffee pot, and the microwave to the dining room to reduce the problems lack of accessibility to remodeled rooms brings.

SIGN UP. With any professional, have the facts on paper to legally protect you before, during, and after the work is done. Define the scope of the project and fees as specifically as possible. The contract should include a clear description of the work to be done, materials that will be required, and who will supply them. It should also spell out commencement and completion dates and any provisions relating to timeliness. It should also include your total costs (subject to additions and deductions by a written change order only). Payments should be tied to work stages; be wary of any contractor who wants a lot of money up front. If ordering certain materials needs to be done weeks in advance (to allow time for manufacturing), then get a list of all those materials and their cost before committing to the idea of up-front money.

TYPICAL COST BREAKDOWN (500-SQ.-FT. ADDITION)

Permit fees	$200
Site preparation and storage	800
Foundation	3,200
Floor framing and subfloor	2,400
Wall framing and sheathing	3,000
Roof framing and sheathing	2,200
Roofing and gutters	1,800
Siding and exterior trim	2,400
Windows and doors	2,000
Exterior painting	2,200
Demolition	1,000
Rough wiring	2,800
Insulation	1,400
Finish walls and ceilings	3,600
Finish electrical	1,400
Heating	3,600
Trim and moldings	1,600
Interior painting	1,800
Floor covering	3,000
Debris removal	1,000
Contingencies	1,200
Subtotal	42,600
Overhead, profit (15 percent)	6,400
TOTAL	**$49,000**

SCHEDULING THE WORK

Here are the major tasks in building an addition, in the order in which they usually occur:

PLANNING AND PREPARATION
- Finalize plans.
- Estimate costs.
- Arrange financing.
- Obtain permits.
- Order materials with long delivery lead times.
- Line up subcontractors.

FOUNDATION
- Lay out building lines.
- Excavate site.
- Build forms; have them inspected.
- Complete foundation.

SHELL (EXTERIOR)
- Frame floor system.
- Install underfloor utilities.
- Have utilities inspected.
- Install subflooring.
- Frame walls and roof.
- Modify common wall.
- Install sheathing.
- Install mechanical ducts.
- Install plumbing and gas lines.
- Install rough wiring, including recessed fixtures.
- Have utility installations and framing inspected.
- Apply roofing.
- Install windows and doors.
- Install siding.

INTERIOR
- Frame interior walls.
- Install insulation and have it inspected.
- Apply wallboard and have it inspected.
- Finish wall surface.
- Install trim.
- Hang doors.
- Paint interior and exterior.
- Install floor underlayment.
- Install cabinets, shelves, and countertops.
- Install plumbing fixtures.
- Install built-in appliances.
- Install electrical fixtures.
- Install finish flooring.
- Install freestanding appliances (refrigerator, range).
- Complete trim and decorative details.

COMPLETION
- Get final inspections.
- Convert construction loan.

PROJECT MANAGEMENT

PLANS

The most important element in a successful building project is a set of construction drawings—the plans. Good plans help you picture the project before you begin and serve as a valuable reference throughout the project. Complete and well-thought-out plans will help you estimate material and labor costs accurately. The plans will also show subcontractors exactly what you want so they can submit accurate bids. You'll need good plans, too, to secure project financing and obtain necessary permits.

You can draw plans yourself or hire an architect, usually for about 15 percent of the project cost. Many lumberyards or home centers will help, too. Expecting that you will buy most of your building materials there, the supplier will translate your rough sketches into a minimal, but acceptable, set of plans.

If you draw your own plans, have them checked by experienced building professionals to ensure that the project meets building codes, its structural elements are properly sized, and you haven't overlooked any crucial elements. Local building code authorities will review your plans, too.

WHAT ROLE WILL YOU PLAY?

Some confident and ambitious homeowners tackle the entire project on their own, while others prefer to hand the plans to a general contractor, who then does the job. Between these extremes, you can do some of the work yourself and contract the rest or act as your own general contractor, hiring and managing subcontractors to do the complete job.

DOING IT YOURSELF: There are two reasons for building an addition yourself—to have the pleasure and pride of building your own home or to save money. How much money you can save depends on your skills and how many special tools you will have to rent or buy.

Here are some ways to cut costs by doing work yourself:

■ Do the work of the highest paid building professionals—usually skilled workers, such as plumbers and electricians.

■ Do the tasks that have high labor cost relative to material cost, such as insulating, shingling, roofing, and painting.

■ Do the small jobs that would take a professional less than half a day, such as tiling a countertop or installing vinyl flooring.

■ Take charge of selecting and buying materials and having them delivered on time.

TYPICAL COST BREAKDOWN (500-SQ.-FT. ADDITION)

Permit fees	$200
Site preparation and storage	800
Foundation	3,200
Floor framing and subfloor	2,400
Wall framing and sheathing	3,000
Roof framing and sheathing	2,200
Roofing and gutters	1,800
Siding and exterior trim	2,400
Windows and doors	2,000
Exterior painting	2,200
Demolition	1,000
Rough wiring	2,800
Insulation	1,400
Finish walls and ceilings	3,600
Finish electrical	1,400
Heating	3,600
Trim and moldings	1,600
Interior painting	1,800
Floor covering	3,000
Debris removal	1,000
Contingencies	1,200
Subtotal	42,600
Overhead, profit (15 percent)	6,400
TOTAL	**$49,000**

ACTING AS THE CONTRACTOR: Managing a construction project is like running a small business—you have to plan and schedule work, make decisions about every detail, negotiate with a number of people, understand each task and how it relates to others, manage the finances, and pay the bills.

This will always require much more time than you expect. You'll spend a lot of time negotiating with subcontractors and suppliers. If you already have a full schedule, you will have to eliminate some things to manage your additional project.

To succeed as a project manager, you must be organized, clear about the details of your project, and prepared to spend long hours on the telephone. You'll need to set a budget and adhere to it and make payments to suppliers and subcontractors on time. It helps if you have a lot of patience and good humor.

HIRING A CONTRACTOR: If you decide to have a general contractor oversee the project, you will first have to find a reputable contractor who will work with you and stick to his estimate (unless you approve changes). You must be responsive when dealing with the contractor, and make decisions quickly and firmly when requested by your contractor.

ESTIMATING THE COSTS

An important step in construction, before the first nail is driven, is estimating the cost. If you hire a general contractor or subcontractors, their bids will be your estimates. If you do the job yourself, you will have to make your own cost estimate.

There are two kinds of costs to consider in your estimate: predictable and hidden.

To estimate predictable costs, break the project into smaller parts, such as foundation work, framing, and roofing, then estimate the material and labor costs for each part.

A construction cost estimating book, available at bookstores, will help you make a preliminary estimate of predictable costs. These books show customary time and material requirements for every step in the construction process, including per-square-foot costs for typical floors, walls, ceilings, and other basic items. They also give regional adjustment factors for material and labor costs. Since they are based on costs submitted by builders, they are accurate for normal construction. The cost breakdown for a 500-square-foot, single-story addition of average quality on the opposite page was developed from a cost estimating book.

Hidden costs are harder to estimate; they arise from the surprises that inevitably occur during a project. Take time to imagine what situations could lead to changes in your plans, then include best-guess costs for them. Hidden costs often include:

- liability insurance
- repairs or changes to the existing house
- debris removal and dump fees
- power cords or temporary power
- tool purchases, rentals, and replacements
- blade sharpening and replacement
- electric-service upgrades
- underground utility changes
- matching old or obsolete materials
- inability to recycle materials as expected
- landscape repairs or replacement

When you have your final plans, itemize the materials and get firm price quotations from suppliers. Be sure to include easily overlooked items such as nails, hardware, plumbing fixtures, and finishing materials. These costs, along with bids from subcontractors, will give you a more complete cost estimate.

PREPARING YOURSELF

A building and remodeling project is noisy, hectic, and wearing. Be prepared for setbacks, disruptions, conflicts, and constant mess. You'll tolerate it best when you enjoy the building process and the job's progress. And always try to remain cool when the inevitable snags occur.

Minimize clutter on the job by clearing out your garage, yard, or patio and devoting the space to material storage and preparation. Combat stress by setting aside part of your budget—in money and time—for occasional dinners out or weekend getaways.

SCHEDULING THE WORK

Here are the major tasks in building an addition, in the order in which they usually occur:

PLANNING AND PREPARATION
Finalize plans.
Estimate costs.
Arrange financing.
Obtain permits.
Order materials with long delivery
   lead times.
Line up subcontractors.
FOUNDATION
Lay out building lines.
Excavate site.
Build forms; have them inspected.
Complete foundation.
SHELL (EXTERIOR)
Frame floor system.
Install underfloor utilities.
Have utilities inspected.
Install subflooring.

Frame walls and roof.
Modify common wall.
Install sheathing.
Install mechanical ducts.
Install plumbing and gas lines.
Install rough wiring, including
   recessed fixtures.
Have utility installations and
   framing inspected.
Apply roofing.
Install windows and doors.
Install siding.
INTERIOR
Frame interior walls.
Install insulation and have
   it inspected.
Apply wallboard and have
   it inspected.

Finish wall surface.
Install trim.
Hang doors.
Paint interior and exterior.
Install floor underlayment.
Install cabinets, shelves,
   and countertops.
Install plumbing fixtures.
Install built-in appliances.
Install electrical fixtures.
Install finish flooring.
Install freestanding appliances
   (refrigerator, range).
Complete trim and decorative details.
COMPLETION
Get final inspections.
Convert construction loan.

FOUNDATIONS

A foundation's main functions include:
■ supporting the building and anchoring it against wind
■ preventing vertical frost heave
■ isolating the building from the ground

Some other common functions include:
■ protecting against termites
■ protecting from heat loss and storing the building's heat in winter
■ absorbing excess heat in summer
■ providing space for storage, mechanical systems, and additional living areas

TYPES OF FOUNDATIONS

FULL BASEMENT: In deep-frost areas, excavate for a full basement, when possible. (To avoid undermining the existing foundation, dig a full basement for an addition only when the house already has a basement or deep footings.) A full basement puts the footings below the frost line and helps protect the plumbing from freezing. The floor slab and wall footings are poured concrete; the walls may be concrete or blocks.

PERIMETER WALL: A full basement might not be practical where the water table is high. A shorter perimeter wall, constructed the same way, is economical and provides the same benefits, except headroom.

SLAB ON GRADE: This economical foundation allows you to finish the foundation and floor in one operation. It also keeps the floor close to the ground—an advantage if height is a problem or if the floor must match an existing slab.

PIER AND GRADE-BEAM: Reinforced concrete beams supported by concrete piers set deep into the ground are used for structures on steep hillsides or unstable soil. They usually require professional engineering. Forms for the beams are built on grade, over the piers, and follow the contour of the slope.

ALL-WEATHER WOOD FOUNDATION: Full-basement and perimeter-wall foundations of pressure-treated lumber and plywood have been used in Canada for 50 years. These foundations require proper materials, assembly, and backfilling techniques, so seek advice from an architect or foundation contractor who specializes in them.

A DO-IT-YOURSELF JOB?

Unless you have experience in foundation work, hire a subcontractor. Building a foundation is heavy, backbreaking work that comes at the beginning of your project, when you might not be in shape nor have full confidence in your building skills. The foundation establishes the dimensions and levelness of the building that sits on top of it, so it must be constructed with dimensions accurate to ¼ inch. You can make adjustments in any other part of the building as you work, but concrete is permanent.

You may be able to save some money on the foundation even if you don't do the whole job. A contractor might lower the price if you can correctly do some simple but time-consuming tasks such as laying out the foundation perimeter lines and building the batter boards, scheduling the excavator, placing the perimeter drains, waterproofing the walls, placing exterior insulation (if any), or backfilling around the foundation.

TYPES OF FOUNDATIONS

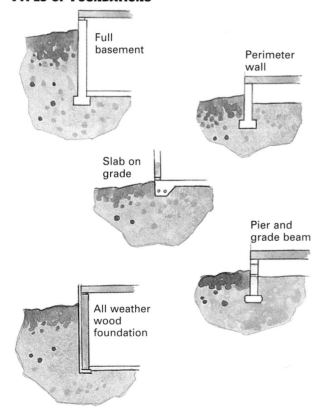

Full basement

Perimeter wall

Slab on grade

Pier and grade beam

All weather wood foundation

ANTICIPATING REQUIREMENTS

Projects are always easier when you anticipate special needs and problems before they occur. Run through the Excavation and Special Tools checklists on the opposite page to make sure you are ready to start your foundation, whether you use a subcontractor or not.

EXCAVATION: Hire an excavation contractor to dig the foundation and footing trenches (with the possible exception of a small slab on grade) and the hole for a full basement. Ask your foundation contractor which excavator he would prefer to do the digging. If it is someone he works with often, ask him to coordinate the digging and the placing of forms.

Here are some problems you might have to solve before digging begins:

■ Are there any obstructions, such as trees, utility lines, septic tanks, or old footings that will make excavation difficult? You might have to remove one or more trees (the excavator will remove the stumps). Call the utility company to move service wires.

■ Are there any nuisance plants, such as poison oak or berry bushes, that you should remove before laying out the lines?

■ Can a backhoe, concrete mixer, or other large equipment get to the site? If not, can you remove a section of fence or get permission to pass through a neighbor's yard?

■ Is there room to store lumber, steel reinforcing, gravel, crushed stone, sand, concrete blocks, and other bulky material?

Where will it be delivered? How will it get to your site?

■ Where will the excavated dirt go? Even a modest trench yields an astonishing pile of soil. If you don't have room in your own yard, ask your neighbors and friends if they would like some free fill, or look into public landfills. Your excavator will probably know someone who will take the fill.

■ Will a deep excavation or pier holes create a safety hazard for children? Be ready to put up a temporary railing around the excavation or cover deep bores with plywood.

SPECIAL TOOLS: Foundation work requires some special tools:

■ A water level, builder's level, or transit for leveling widely separated points. (For small additions, you can use a level and a long, straight board.)

■ Two good wheelbarrows or a rented conveyor for hand digging.

■ A long-handle, square-nose shovel for trimming trench bottoms.

■ A rebar cutter/bender. For a small job, you can cut rebar with a hacksaw or reciprocating saw and bend no. 3 or no. 4 rebar by hand against a firm object.

■ A hammer drill for drilling holes into the existing foundation.

■ Concrete finishing tools for slab work (wood or magnesium floats, a tamper, a bull float, a fresno, a seamer, and a steel trowel).

■ Tools for block work (a trowel, a 4-foot level, and a joint finisher).

CODE REQUIREMENTS

GRADING
The backfill around a foundation must be graded to slope away at a minimum of 6 inches in 10 feet on all sides.

FOOTINGS
Footings must be level on the top surface with a maximum slope of 10 percent on the bottom surface; step the footings where the slope exceeds 10 percent.

CONCRETE FLOORS ON GROUND
Remove all vegetation, topsoil, and foreign material. Maximum depth of clean and compacted fill:
■ earth—8 inches
■ sand or gravel—24 inches
Below-grade base courses, except on well-drained soil or a sand-gravel mixture, must be clean sand, gravel, crushed stone, or slag 4 inches thick.
A vapor barrier is required under slabs except for:
■ detached, unheated structures
■ when excepted by code official

PROTECTION AGAINST DECAY
Use pressure-treated wood for these parts:
■ joists up to 18 inches above grade within a foundation
■ girders up to 12 inches above grade within foundation
■ sills or plates on concrete up to 8 inches above grade
■ siding or sheathing up to 6 inches above grade
■ basement wall furring strips without a vapor barrier
■ sills and sleepers on a slab without a vapor barrier
■ posts and columns in direct contact with the ground or embedded in concrete and exposed to the weather

ANCHOR BOLTS
Embed ½-inch anchor bolts 15 inches into masonry or 7 inches into concrete; space them 6 feet on-center and no more than 12 inches from corners.

CRAWLSPACE VENT OPENINGS
■ net vent area without vapor barrier: $\frac{1}{150}$ floor area
■ net vent area with vapor barrier: $\frac{1}{1,500}$ floor area
■ vent opening within 3 feet of each corner
■ corrosion-resistant ⅛-inch mesh screens

CONCRETE FORMS

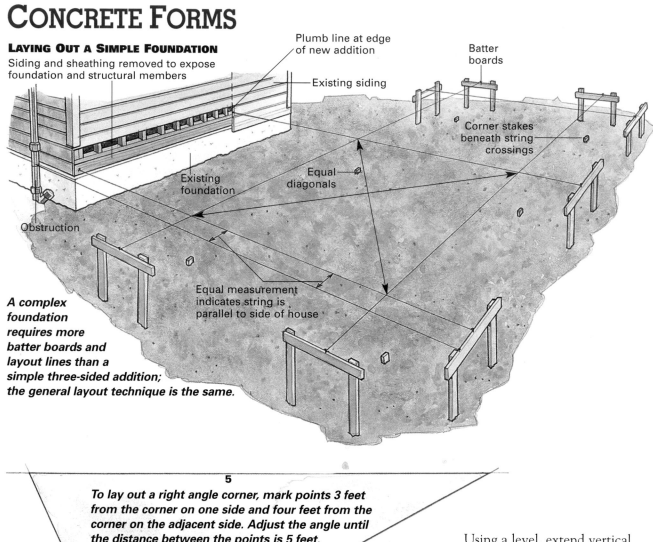

LAYING OUT A SIMPLE FOUNDATION

Siding and sheathing removed to expose foundation and structural members

Plumb line at edge of new addition

Existing siding

Batter boards

Corner stakes beneath string crossings

Existing foundation

Equal diagonals

Obstruction

Equal measurement indicates string is parallel to side of house

A complex foundation requires more batter boards and layout lines than a simple three-sided addition; the general layout technique is the same.

To lay out a right angle corner, mark points 3 feet from the corner on one side and four feet from the corner on the adjacent side. Adjust the angle until the distance between the points is 5 feet. You can use multiples of 3, 4, and 5 for greater accuracy.

5

3

4

90°

LAYING OUT THE FOUNDATION

Set up string lines to establish the outside edges of the foundation wall. Run them between the house and temporary batter boards, which can be taken down and put back up as needed until the foundation is completed. Before you set up the lines, make sure your addition conforms to the setback limits for your property. Your local building inspection department may require a certified survey.

The following procedure describes laying out a simple rectangular addition, but the same technique can be expanded to lay out more complex additions, also.

1. Mark where the outside edges of the new foundation will meet the house foundation.

Using a level, extend vertical lines onto the house siding.

Draw a second line outside each of the foundation lines, separated from it by a distance equal to the thickness of the siding that will be on the addition.

2. Remove some house siding and sheathing between the marks to expose the floor joists and subfloor. Use a circular saw with the blade set deep enough to cut through the siding and sheathing but not into the framing.

3. Measure down from the top of the existing subfloor at both marks to locate the top of the new foundation. Since the dimensions of new and old joists, the mudsill, subflooring, and other members might be different, the tops of the foundations might be at different levels.

4. Drive a nail into the house framing or a cleat attached to the house at each point. Attach a nylon mason's line to each nail. Check the lines with a level; if they are not level, lower the string at the higher corner. You can adjust for the difference later when you frame the floor.

5. Build batter boards at one outer corner 6 feet beyond the corner of the addition so they will not interfere with the excavation. To build them, drive two pairs of pointed 2×4s into the ground about 4 feet apart, as shown above. Center them on the corner. Screw a level crosspiece to the back of the 2×4s facing the house. Place the crosspiece so that the string line attached to the house runs level across the top.

6. Stretch the string line taut across the top of the batter board. Slide it right or left until it is square to the house, then drive a nail into the batter board at that point. Use a 3-4-5 triangle (two legs of 3 and 4 feet, and a hypotenuse of 5 feet) to square the line to the house, as shown on the opposite page. For even greater accuracy, use multiples of 3-4-5, such as 9-12-15 feet or 12-16-20 feet.

7. Build batter boards for the second corner and attach the string. Pull the second string line to its batter board and move it right or left until the two lines are an equal distance apart at both ends.

8. Stretch a third string line between the two side sets of batter boards, intersecting the first pair of lines at the corners of the new foundation.

9. To make sure the string lines are square, measure diagonals and adjust lines until diagonal measurements are within ¼ inch of each other. If your house walls are out of square at a corner where you will attach your addition, the extended wall might look crooked if you lay out the string lines perfectly square. If the wall is not prominent, lay out the lines as described, and conceal the bend in the wall with tall plants.

It's better to align a more prominent addition wall with the existing house wall, even if one wall of the addition will be out of square with the end of the house. To do this, follow the layout procedures described before, but align the first string line with the side of the house. To make sure it is perfectly aligned with the house wall, stretch a new string line along the entire length of that wall, from batter board to the front of house. Move it out far enough to clear any obstructions along the house wall, making sure it is an equal distance from the house foundation at all points. Adjust the line from the foundation so it is parallel to the longer line.

WATER TUBE LEVEL

Mark corners at water level

CONCRETE FORMS
continued

SLAB FOUNDATION

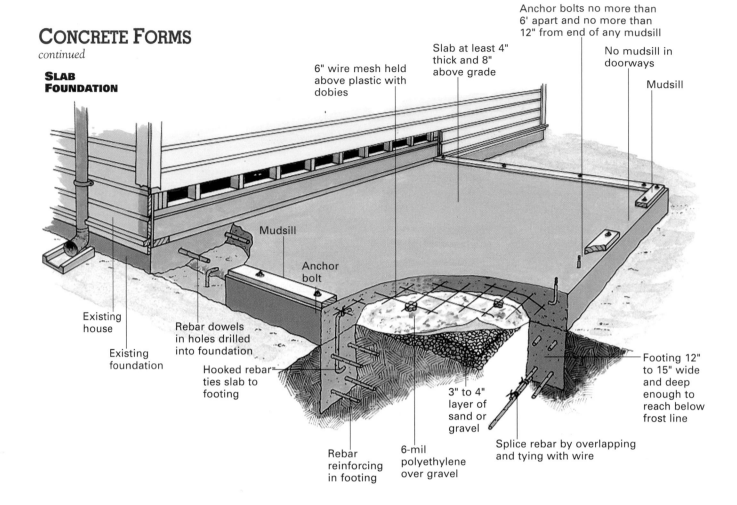

Anchor bolts no more than 6' apart and no more than 12" from end of any mudsill

Slab at least 4" thick and 8" above grade

No mudsill in doorways

Mudsill

6" wire mesh held above plastic with dobies

Mudsill

Anchor bolt

Existing house

Existing foundation

Rebar dowels in holes drilled into foundation

Hooked rebar ties slab to footing

Rebar reinforcing in footing

6-mil polyethylene over gravel

3" to 4" layer of sand or gravel

Splice rebar by overlapping and tying with wire

Footing 12" to 15" wide and deep enough to reach below frost line

EXCAVATION

The excavation contractor will probably paint the layout lines on the ground with a spray can, remove the strings, and start digging. The plans will show the distance from the top of the foundation to the bottom of the slab and footings.

The bottom of the trench for the footings should be level and the sides straight. Do not throw dirt back into the trench; its bottom and sides must be undisturbed soil.

For a full basement foundation, the excavator usually digs to the bottom of the floor slab first, making sure it's level. The footing trenches are then dug. After digging, reset the string lines to build forms.

BUILDING FORMS

SLAB FOUNDATION: The slab and footings are usually formed and poured together, following these steps:
1. Build forms for the slab with 2× lumber held by stakes every 2 feet. Align the forms with string lines, and level the top at least 8 inches above final grade. The trench walls serve as the forms for the footings.

2. Dig trenches for pipes that will run under the slab. Lay the pipes, then backfill.
3. Spread 3 to 4 inches of sand or crushed stone inside the slab perimeter, and cover it with 6-mil polyethylene sheeting as a vapor barrier. Put 2 inches of sand over the sheet.
4. Lay horizontal rebar in the trenches, resting the bottom bars on dobies (small concrete blocks) and suspending the top bars with tie wire hooked onto the top of the form. Tie vertical rebar onto horizontal bars.
5. Lay 6-inch wire mesh over the sand on 2-inch dobies spaced 4 feet apart. Tie the mesh to the rebar in the trench. (You may be able to use fiberglass reinforcement; ask your local code officials and concrete supplier.)
6. Pour the concrete. Fill the footing trenches, then pour the slab. (See page 36 for details about pouring and finishing a slab.) Insert anchor bolts around the perimeter.

Where deeper footings are required, the slab and footings are poured separately. If the slab will rest on the footings, the trenches are adequate for footing forms. Lay rebar in the trenches and pour the concrete. Stand lengths of rebar with hooks formed on one end in the fresh concrete to tie the footing and the slab together. Then build a slab form.

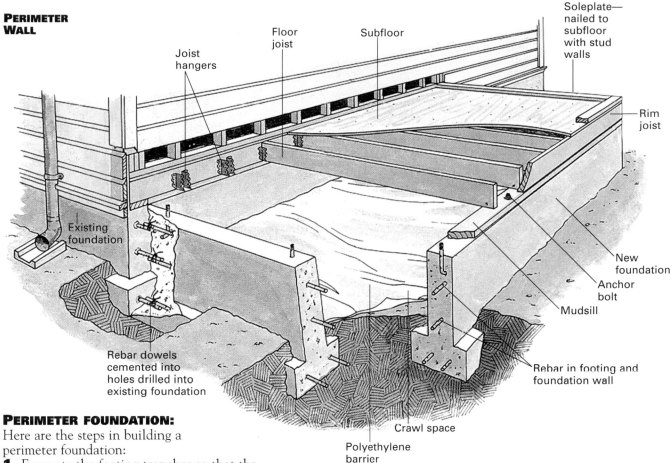

PERIMETER WALL

Joist hangers

Floor joist

Subfloor

Soleplate— nailed to subfloor with stud walls

Rim joist

Existing foundation

New foundation

Anchor bolt

Mudsill

Rebar dowels cemented into holes drilled into existing foundation

Rebar in footing and foundation wall

Crawl space

Polyethylene barrier

PERIMETER FOUNDATION:

Here are the steps in building a perimeter foundation:

1. Excavate the footing trenches so that the foundation wall (which will be narrower than the footings and centered on them) will align with the string lines. The trenches will be the forms for the footings.

2. Rent plywood forms or construct forms of 2× lumber. (You can reuse the lumber for floor joists.) Drive tall stakes into the bottom of the trench every 3 feet, set so the inside faces of the forms will be 8 inches apart.

3. Nail the boards to the stakes for one side of the forms. Level the tops of form boards with the string lines, and place the bottoms high enough to clear the footings. Then, set the rebar in place. Rest the bottom rebar on dobies and fasten all rebar securely with tie wire. Then complete the forms.

4. Insert metal form ties (available at lumberyards and home centers) between the form sides to prevent the concrete from forcing them apart. The ties allow you to free the sides after the concrete sets.

5. Mark locations for ½×10-inch anchor bolts on forms.

6. An intermediate girder is usually required for joist spans over 16 feet. Note where you'll need posts and dig footings for 18×18×12-inch piers at these points. Build simple box forms at least 8 inches square and 8 inches

tall to center over the footing holes. Pour each pier and footing together and insert a post anchor into the wet concrete.

To hold each end of the girder, form pockets in the walls or pour pilasters (columns adjacent to a wall). See Beam Pockets and Pilasters, page 31, for details.

PERIMETER WALL FORM

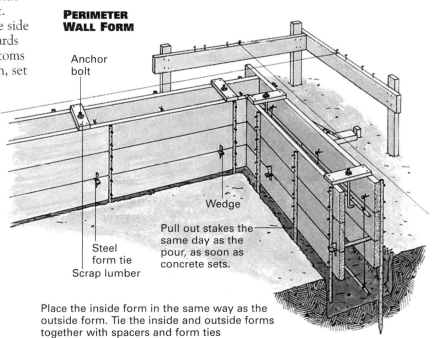

Anchor bolt

Steel form tie

Scrap lumber

Wedge

Pull out stakes the same day as the pour, as soon as concrete sets.

Place the inside form in the same way as the outside form. Tie the inside and outside forms together with spacers and form ties

CONCRETE FORMS
continued

FULL-BASEMENT FOOTING

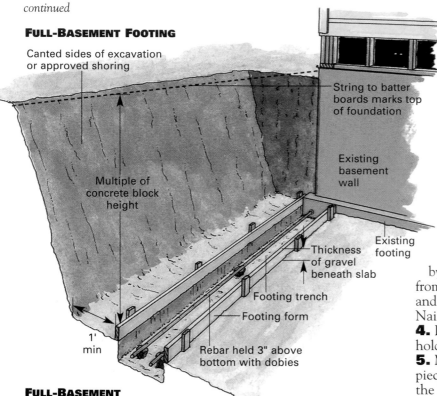

Canted sides of excavation or approved shoring

String to batter boards marks top of foundation

Multiple of concrete block height

Existing basement wall

Thickness of gravel beneath slab

Existing footing

Footing trench

Footing form

Rebar held 3" above bottom with dobies

1' min

FULL-BASEMENT FOUNDATION:

Only a professional should build forms and pour concrete for a full-basement foundation. But, you can build block basement walls on poured footings. Here are the steps.

1. Dig 8 inches below floor level to allow enough depth for a 4-inch slab and 4 inches of gravel.

2. Dig footings wide enough to support the slab after the wall is finished (see below).

3. Build forms along the lip of trench with 2× lumber. Set the height of the footing by measuring a distance divisible by 8 inches (the height of a block) down from string lines. Level the tops of the forms and secure them with 1×2 stakes every 2 feet. Nail 1×2 ties across the top of the forms.

4. Place horizontal rebar in the forms, holding it off the ground with 3-inch dobies.

5. Mark locations on the form boards for pieces of vertical rebar. Lay out the marks so the bars will extend into the holes in the

FULL-BASEMENT BLOCK WALL

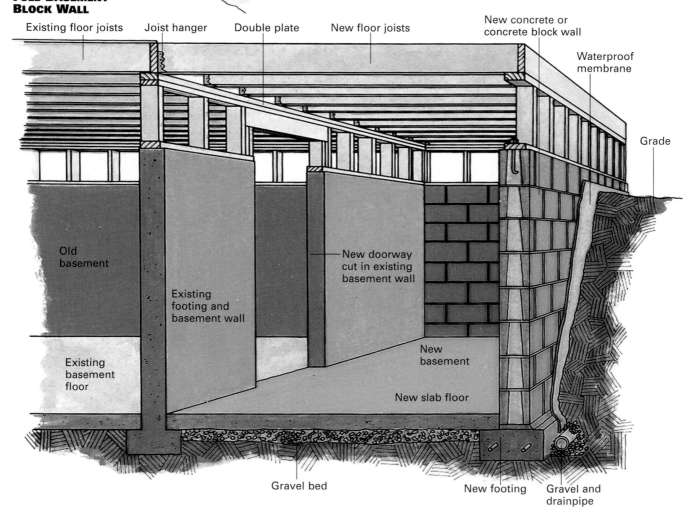

Existing floor joists　Joist hanger　Double plate　New floor joists

New concrete or concrete block wall

Waterproof membrane

Grade

Old basement

Existing footing and basement wall

New doorway cut in existing basement wall

New basement

Existing basement floor

New slab floor

Gravel bed

New footing

Gravel and drainpipe

blocks. You can buy the bars precut, usually with a hook formed at the bottom. Embed the bars in the concrete when it is poured; do not drive them into the ground.

BEAM POCKETS AND PILASTERS: Girders are large beams that bridge from one foundation wall to another, dividing the building into manageable joist spans. The maximum joist span is usually 16 feet; 12 feet will result in a stronger floor.

To support the ends of a girder, either form beam pockets into the foundation walls or pour pilasters—pillars adjacent to the wall—as part of the foundation.

To form a beam pocket, nail two scraps of 2× framing material to the inside of the wall-form boards. A single thickness—1½ inches— is not sufficient because building codes require a bearing surface of at least 3 inches on concrete.

To form a pilaster in a poured-concrete wall, interrupt the line of form boards with an opening 12 inches wide extending from the top of the footing to the point on the top form board where the bottom of the girder will rest. Allow an extra 1½ inches for the thickness of the sill plate on which the joists will rest. Build a box form around the opening, extending out from the wall at least 8 inches.

To form a pilaster in a concrete block foundation, interlock the pilaster blocks with the main wall, and cast rebar in the pilaster block cores. The center of the girder might not fall exactly in the middle of a standard 8-inch block, so build the pilaster two blocks wide.

Support the girder between the walls with wood, steel, or concrete posts. Set the posts on top of 18×18×12-inch footings. The footings can be poured separately or together with the floor slab.

BEAM POCKET/POCKET FOR GIRDER

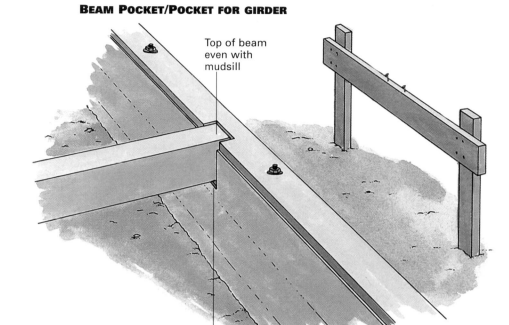

Top of beam even with mudsill

Aluminum flashing or roofing felt keeps the beam from contact with concrete

PILASTERS IN BLOCK WALL

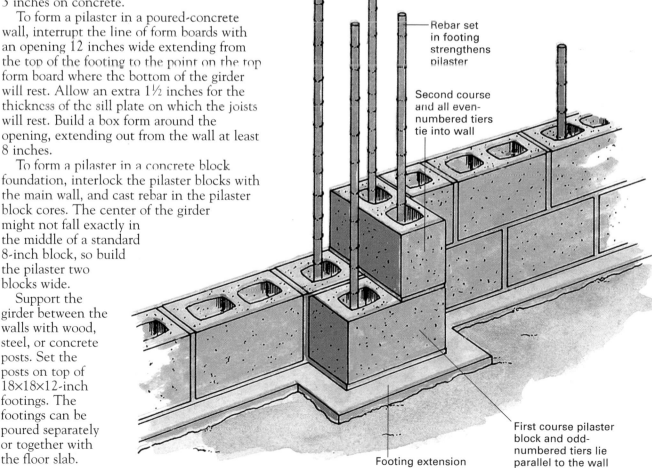

Rebar set in footing strengthens pilaster

Second course and all even-numbered tiers tie into wall

First course pilaster block and odd-numbered tiers lie parallel to the wall

Footing extension

CONCRETE FORMS
continued

GRADE-BEAM FOUNDATION: A grade-beam foundation requires less excavation and uses less concrete than a perimeter wall, yet it looks and functions like one. It is, in fact, a shallow perimeter wall supported by piers that reach below the frost line or through unstable soil. It serves well where frost penetrates to a great depth or where the ground slopes. Here is how to construct a grade beam:

1. Locate the centers for the supporting piers uniformly around the foundation, no more than 8 feet on-center. Place piers adjacent to the existing foundation and at each corner. Mark the centers on the layout strings with pieces of tape or yarn.

2. Excavate for the footings that will support the piers. The bottoms of the footings must extend below the maximum frost depth and below any unstable soil. The footings should be 18 inches square (or equivalent area) and at least 8 inches thick. Dig the holes by hand or hire an excavator with a power auger.

3. Drive two reinforcing rods into the soil where they will stand at least 3 inches inside the edges of the piers to be formed on top of the footings. The rebar should be long enough to project at least 24 inches above grade.

4. Pour the footings.

5. Place 8-inch-diameter form tubes (cylindrical paper forms) atop the footings, enclosing the rebar. The tops of the tubes should be at grade level.

6. Carefully backfill around the form tubes without moving them. Don't let any soil fall into the tubes.

7. Build forms for the beams across the tops of the form tubes. They will be like forms for a perimeter wall, except the earth at grade becomes the bottom of the form. The beam must be at least 2 feet high at all points. On a slope, keep the bottoms of the forms level by stepping them in 1-foot increments.

8. Lay horizontal rebar in the forms as shown for perimeter walls (see page 30). Bend the vertical bars from the piers at right angles, and tie them to the bottom bars in the beam, overlapping by at least 20 inches.

9. Mark locations for $\frac{1}{2}\times10$-inch anchor bolts on forms.

10. Mark the height of the concrete on the inside of the form wall so that you can bring it to the right level as you pour.

11. Pour the concrete. Consolidate it with a shovel or vibrator, then screed the top surface level.

12. When the concrete begins to set, place the anchor bolts, standing them straight.

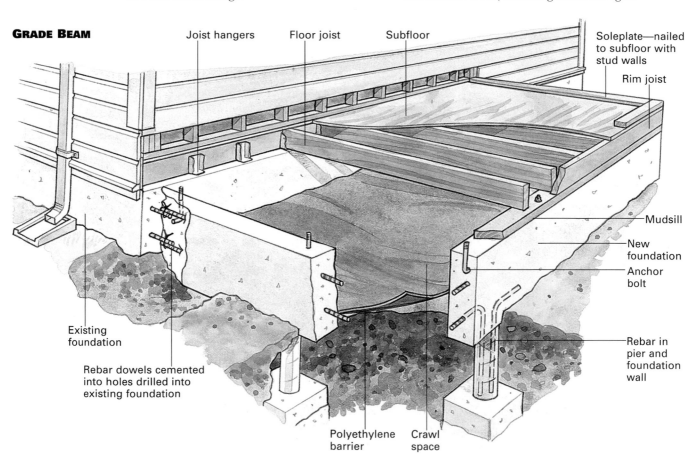

GRADE BEAM — Joist hangers · Floor joist · Subfloor · Soleplate—nailed to subfloor with stud walls · Rim joist · Mudsill · New foundation · Anchor bolt · Rebar in pier and foundation wall · Crawl space · Polyethylene barrier · Rebar dowels cemented into holes drilled into existing foundation · Existing foundation

ALL-WEATHER WOOD FOUNDATION

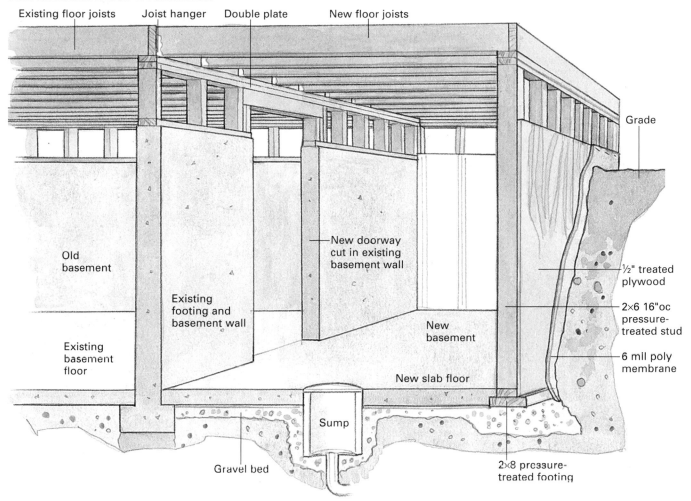

Existing floor joists   Joist hanger   Double plate   New floor joists

Grade

Old basement

New doorway cut in existing basement wall

Existing footing and basement wall

New basement

½" treated plywood

2×6 16"oc pressure-treated stud

Existing basement floor

New slab floor

6 mil poly membrane

Sump

Gravel bed

2×8 pressure-treated footing

ALL-WEATHER WOOD FOUNDATION:

Wood-framed walls withstand ground movement better than concrete walls because they will flex slightly rather than crack. This—plus the ease of finishing the interior—makes wood-framed walls ideal for a full-basement foundation.

Many people shy away from a wood foundation, knowing that wood will rot in contact with the earth. But pressure-treated wood won't rot when in ground contact. Treated wood has been used for foundations for more than 50 years. Ask a professional familiar with wood foundations for design advice. Here is the general construction procedure, which also applies to building a wood perimeter wall:

1. Excavate a level basement hole 7 inches deeper than the final slab or floor surface.
2. Excavate for a sump pit and drainage pipe. Or, dig just the pit and install a sump pump.
3. Install a 24-inch-diameter precast concrete tile with removable cover for the sump. Place the cover flush with the finish slab surface.
4. Pour 4 inches of pea gravel over the floor area and around the tile. Level the gravel.

5. Lay a 6-mil polyethylene membrane over the gravel, overlapping seams by 24 inches.
6. Lay pressure-treated 2×8s around the perimeter as a footing for the wood wall.
7. Frame the wood walls with pressure-treated 2×6 studs, 16 inches on-center.
8. Sheath the outside of the walls with pressure-treated ½-inch plywood. The face grain should be vertical. Make sure all joints are on studs.
9. Install the floor system above to stabilize the tops of the walls.
10. Pour a 3-inch floor slab flush with the tops of the wall bottom plates. Reinforce the slab with either 6×6 welded-wire mesh or fiberglass strands added to the concrete.
11. Staple a continuous sheet of 6-mil polyethylene to the wall top plate so that it hangs down over the outside of the plywood to the bottom of the wall.
12. Apply a protective finish (painted exterior plywood or fiberglass-reinforced and latex-modified mortar) to the portion of the wall that will remain above grade.
13. Backfill against the wall. Grade the soil to slope away from the foundation at a minimum of 6 inches in 10 feet.

WORKING WITH CONCRETE

ORDERING CONCRETE

Unless you need such a small amount of concrete that you can mix it by hand, order a ready-mixed concrete delivery. If the ready-mix truck can't drive to your addition site, you will also need to hire a concrete-pumping service or enlist several strong helpers with wheelbarrows. Of course, if you have hired a contractor to pour your foundation, the contractor will order the concrete and provide the labor for placement.

When ordering concrete, you must estimate the amount and specify the kind of concrete mix you want. Here are some pointers on ordering concrete:

FIGURING HOW MUCH TO ORDER:

Concrete is sold by the cubic yard, usually just called a yard. A cubic yard is the volume of a cube that measures 3×3×3 feet, or 27 cubic feet. Figure the amount of concrete needed for footings, walls, slabs, and walks from the tables below left. Add 10 percent to your estimate to allow for spreading of the forms and waste.

Most ready-mix concrete companies set the delivery minimum at 1 cubic yard. Many add an additional charge for orders less than 5 or 6 yards. You won't have to take the whole minimum yard when it's delivered, but you will have to pay for it. If you don't need the whole yard, consider having forms ready so you can pour a sidewalk, footings for a deck, or even concrete pavers with the excess.

AGGREGATE SIZE: Use ¾-inch aggregate for most projects, unless building codes require a different size. If you will have the concrete pumped, check with the pumping company to make sure its equipment will handle the size of aggregate you are using.

CEMENT CONTENT: You must specify the number of bags of cement per yard of concrete. A five-bag mix is normally requested when the aggregate is ¾ inch. A six-bag mix is recommended for ⅜-inch aggregate or when higher-strength concrete is needed.

OTHER FACTORS: You may also need to specify water-to-cement ratio (1 to 2 by weight is standard for residential foundations), slump (4 inches for most jobs; 6 inches for filling concrete block), and air entrainment (a treatment for cold weather that helps prevent frost damage, usually specified as 6 percent).

You might also have to pay a standby charge for time the concrete truck remains at your job site, after an allowance for unloading time (usually about 5 minutes per yard). A concrete-pumping service usually charges an hourly fee plus a rate for each yard pumped.

Make sure you are prepared when the ready-mix truck arrives so you won't have to pay the standby charge and to

ESTIMATING CONCRETE FOR FOOTINGS AND WALLS
(CUBIC YARD PER LINEAR FOOT OF FORMS)

Height, inches	Width, inches						
	6	8	10	12	16	20	24
8	.012	.017	.020	.025	.033	.041	.049
12	.019	.025	.031	.037	.049	.062	.074
24	.037	.049	.062	.074	.099	.123	.148
36	.056	.074	.093	.111	.148	.185	.222
48	.074	.098	.124	.148	.198	.246	.296
60	.093	.123	.155	.185	.247	.308	.370
72	.111	.148	.185	.222	.296	.370	.444
84	.130	.173	.216	.259	.345	.432	.518
96	.148	.198	.247	.296	.395	.494	.593

ESTIMATING CONCRETE FOR SLABS AND WALKS
(CUBIC YARDS)

Area, square feet	Thickness, inches						
	2	3	4	5	6	8	10
10	.06	.09	.12	.14	.19	.25	.29
20	.12	.19	.25	.29	.37	.50	.58
50	.31	.47	.62	.72	.93	1.24	1.44
100	.62	.94	1.24	1.44	1.86	2.48	2.88
200	1.2	1.9	2.5	2.9	3.7	5.0	5.8
500	3.1	4.7	6.2	7.2	9.3	12.4	14.4
1,000	6.2	9.4	12.4	14.4	18.6	24.8	28.8

avoid having to add water to the concrete if it begins to set in the truck.

INSTALLING REBAR

Plans for most residential foundations call for no. 4 rebar, which is ½ inch in diameter. This size can be bent and cut fairly easily.

Use a special cutting tool for rebar—which also bends rebar—or cut it with a metal cutoff blade in a circular saw or a metal-cutting blade in a reciprocating saw.

Splice rebar with tie wire. Codes specify that two pieces overlap by at least 40 diameters (20 inches for no. 4 rebar).

Codes also specify concrete cover—the minimum thickness of concrete surrounding rebar. Where concrete is below grade, rebar must be placed at least 3 inches from the ground on all sides. Above grade, the cover must be at least 1½ inches.

Attach rebar for a new foundation to shorter lengths of rebar embedded into the existing foundation. First drill ⅝-inch holes at least 4 inches into the old foundation and blow the dust out. Cut 24-inch lengths of rebar, and cement one into each hole with special epoxy mortar or other compound before you build the forms.

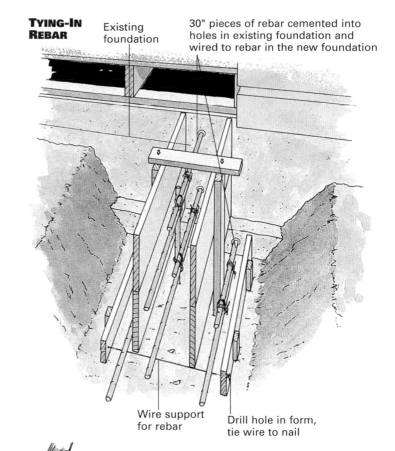

TYING-IN REBAR

Existing foundation

30" pieces of rebar cemented into holes in existing foundation and wired to rebar in the new foundation

Wire support for rebar

Drill hole in form, tie wire to nail

POURING A FORM

Tamp concrete to consolidate it

After the concrete settles, level the top by dragging a screed (a piece of 2×4) across the top of the forms. Use a sawing motion to push excess concrete in front of the screed and fill in low spots behind it. Allow the concrete to stiffen slightly before setting anchor bolts or lengths of vertical rebar in place.

PLACING CONCRETE

On the day of the pour, have plenty of help lined up. As you pump or place concrete, start at the lowest point in the forms. For deep forms, fill the footing area before filling the walls.

Don't handle concrete too much—just enough to get it into place. Then use a rod, shovel, or vibrating machine to consolidate it. Hit the sides of the forms with a hammer to release air pockets.

THUMP THUMP

Strike hammer on stake to spread impact and effect

POURING A SLAB

PREPARING, POURING, AND LEVELING THE SLAB

FINISHING THE SLAB

Level the surface with a magnesium bull float. Push the float with the leading edge raised slightly so it won't dig in.

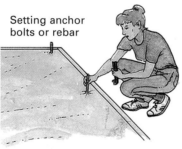

Setting anchor bolts or rebar

After the concrete stiffens slightly, insert anchor bolts or vertical rebar where indicated on the forms.

Finishing the surface

Steel troweling gives the concrete a smooth surface. Wait until the surface water disappears before troweling.

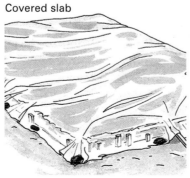

Covered slab

Prevent the concrete from drying too quickly while it cures. Plastic sheeting will trap the moisture to control drying.

A s you pump or pour concrete into forms for a slab, start at the farthest point. When pouring the slab and footings together, fill the footing area and let it stiffen slightly before pouring the slab.

Handle concrete only enough to get it into place. Then use a shovel or vibrating machine to consolidate it.

After the concrete settles, level it by dragging a screed (a piece of 2×4) across the tops of the forms. Use a sawing motion to push excess concrete along in front of the screed and fill in low spots behind it. Let the concrete stiffen slightly before setting anchor bolts or lengths of vertical rebar.

FINISHING THE CONCRETE

After screeding, tamp the concrete with a special tamper so the aggregate settles slightly and a creamy mixture rises to the surface. Then float the slab, using a bull float with a long handle to reach the center. If the slab is larger than 10×16 feet, use a jointer trowel to groove it across the middle to limit cracks. Use a long 2×4 for a straightedge.

After the concrete has stiffened slightly and surface bleed water has evaporated, finish the surface with a steel trowel and set the anchor bolts. If you want a smooth, flat surface, hire a professional finisher.

Cover the slab with polyethylene sheeting for 10 to 14 days to cure. If there is danger of freezing, which can prevent the concrete from setting up properly, cover the plastic with insulating material to hold in heat.

Floating the slab

LAYING CONCRETE BLOCKS

Lay blocks beside the footing excavation, and drive rebars into the middle of the trench every 4 feet, as shown in the illustration at right.

After the footing has cured, place the two corner blocks of the first course. (Always place blocks with the wider webs on top.) Set each block into a layer of mortar and press it down to within ⅜ inch of the footing. Stretch a line between the corner blocks to guide the rest of the first course.

Lay mortar on the footing and apply mortar to one end of each block as you set it in place (called buttering). Raise the buttered end slightly and lower it to fit snugly against the preceding block in one smooth motion. Tap the block level with the trowel handle, then scrape away excess mortar with the blade. Check your work often with a level, both horizontally and vertically.

Fill the cores with concrete after the wall has dried overnight. Even if your plans do not require concrete in every space, you will have to fill cores every 4 to 6 feet for setting anchor bolts. If the code does not require concrete filling, pour insulating material, such as vermiculite, into the cores.

LAYING CONCRETE BLOCK

Rebar driven into bottom of trench in line with the first hole in every fourth block—every 4" with 16" blocks

Dry run of blocks laid beside the footing trench to set the position of rebar

Rebar in footing trench raised at least 2" on stones or pieces of brick

Lay out blocks in a dry run to determine placement of vertical rebar. Place the bars so they will fall in the center of the first core of every fourth block, about 4 feet apart.

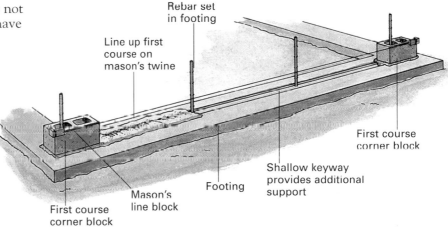

Rebar set in footing

Line up first course on mason's twine

First course corner block

First course corner block

Mason's line block

Footing

Shallow keyway provides additional support

Set the corner blocks for the first course, and stretch a mason's line between them. As you lay the remaining blocks in the course, align them with the line. Don't let them touch the string, however; that could distort the line.

After the first few courses, add additional lengths of rebar by sliding them down the cavity beside the first rod. Tamp the concrete to hold the new rod tightly

Set each block in place and tap it gently to line it up with the string

Add lengths of rebar after a few courses. Slide the new bars into the block cores next to the original rods. Tamp concrete into the cores to hold the new bars securely.

For each new course, stretch a mason's line between the corner blocks to indicate the top of the blocks. As you set each block, align its top edge with the line to ensure a straight, true wall. Check the wall often with a level.

INSULATING FOUNDATION WALLS

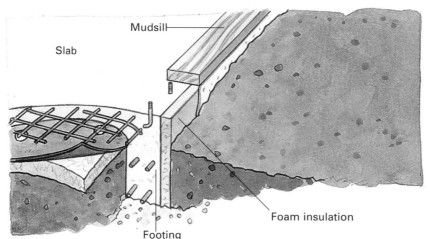

Mudsill

Slab

Foam insulation

Footing

allows you to construct a slab with a shallow footing even in cold northern areas.

Sunlight attacks polystyrene, so you must cover any exposed insulation. Since the bottom of the sheathing and siding must be a minimum of 6 inches above grade, you will have a 6-inch strip to cover. The material that looks most natural (like concrete) is a fiberglass-reinforced, modified latex coating, described on the next page.

SLAB

Concrete conducts heat. To prevent heat loss from the floor to the outside, you have to insulate a slab around its perimeter. Closed-cell, extruded polystyrene is the best material to use because it is impervious to moisture. The insulation should extend to the maximum depth of frost.

To prevent freeze-thaw cycles from lifting the insulation, place the foam inside the footing and slab form before pouring the concrete. The sill plate will extend over the foam and hold it in place, as shown below. After the wall is framed, extend the sheathing slightly over the sill and foam.

Research has shown that insulating to 1 foot below grade and horizontally for a total distance equal to the depth of frost is as effective as insulating straight down. This

PERIMETER WALL

A perimeter wall can be insulated on the outside with foam (explained in the full-basement section that follows) or on the inside with faced fiberglass blanket or batt insulation. To insulate with fiberglass:
1. Lay a polyethylene sheet over the ground inside the wall. Overlap any seams by 1 foot and weight the seams to seal the joints.
2. Cut insulation batts long enough to extend from the sill and at least 1 foot out onto the plastic sheeting, as shown at bottom left.
3. Staple the top of the facing to the edge of the sill, then staple the flanges along the sides of the batts together, forming a continuous layer of insulation over the wall.
4. Weight the bottoms of the batts with scrap pieces of 2×4.
5. Cut blocks of extruded polystyrene or other closed-cell foam board to fit tightly in the spaces between the joists. Press the blocks firmly against the rim joist to eliminate any air space. If the blocks are too loose to stay in place, nail them to the rim joist. Local fire codes may require covering the foam with ½-inch drywall.

You could fill the spaces instead with fiberglass batt. Either trim the fiberglass back 1 inch all around to give you stapling flanges, or install unfaced fiberglass and staple polyethylene sheets to the subfloor, joists, and sill to seal the fiberglass against moisture.

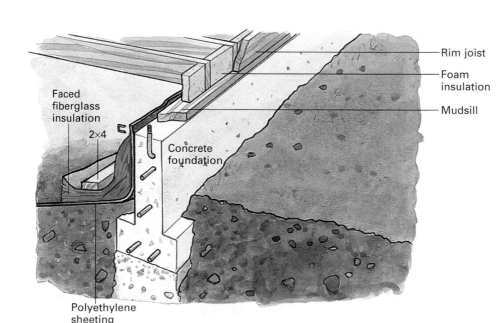

Faced fiberglass insulation

2×4

Concrete foundation

Rim joist

Foam insulation

Mudsill

Polyethylene sheeting

FULL BASEMENT

A concrete or masonry full-basement wall can be insulated either on the inside or the outside, but exterior insulation gives the greatest benefit. Here's why:

■ Enclosing the thermal mass (heat storage capacity) of the concrete within the building's insulation envelope lessens the temperature change of the basement caused by outside temperature changes.

■ Isolating the wall from the cool earth in summer allows it to reach the same temperature as basement air, eliminating condensation and mold.

■ Exterior insulation minimizes the freezing-and-thawing cycle of water in voids and cracks, which damages concrete and concrete-block walls.

Here's how to insulate the outside of a basement wall:

1. Set the concrete forms 2 inches inside the building lines, allowing 2 inches for exterior foam insulation.

2. Before backfilling the basement wall, coat the wall from footing to sill with a nonpetroleum-based moisture barrier (petroleum attacks plastic foams).

3. Apply 1½-inch-thick, tongue-and-groove, extruded polystyrene panels vertically, snugging the panels up under the sill and the lip of the sheathing. Attach the panels with one hardened concrete screw and a plaster button (a large perforated washer for repairing plaster) for each 2-foot-wide panel.

4. Backfill to within 6 inches of final grade.

5. Brush the exposed foam with a steel wire brush to give the foam tooth for the coating to be applied.

6. Cover all screw heads, foam joints, and corners with strips of self-adhesive, fiberglass-mesh drywall tape.

7. Mix fiberglass-reinforced, latex-modified mortar (available at masonry supply outlets) in a 5-gallon pail with a power paint mixer.

8. Brush or trowel the first coat of mortar over the taped areas.

9. After the first coat dries, apply a coat to the entire surface, extending down from the sheathing to 6 inches below final grade.

10. After the mortar cures, finish backfilling. Grade the soil to slope away from the foundation at 6 inches per 10 feet.

11. Fill the gap between the foam and the sheathing, which could be up to ½ inch wide. An easy way to caulk the gap is with foam backer rod, available in ⅛-, ¼-, and ½-inch diameters at lumberyards and home centers. Stuff the rod into the gap with a putty knife.

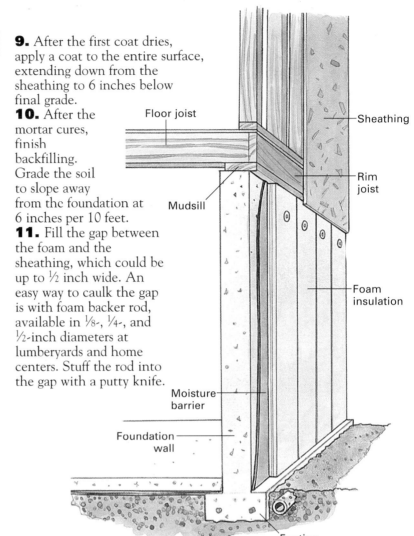

Floor joist
Sheathing
Rim joist
Mudsill
Foam insulation
Moisture barrier
Foundation wall
Footing

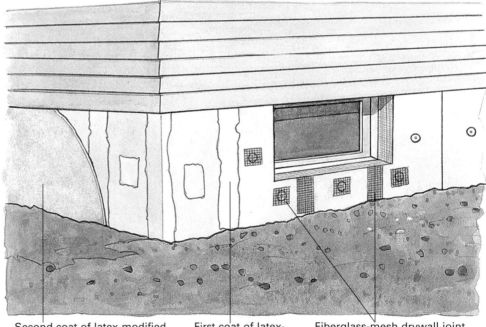

Second coat of latex-modified mortar over foam extends 6 inches below grade

First coat of latex-modified mortar over taped areas

Fiberglass-mesh drywall joint tape over nailheads and joints

BUILDING THE SHELL

THE FLOOR

In most additions, except those built on concrete slabs, the floor consists of subflooring nailed or screwed to joists. The joists rest directly on the mudsill or on a short knee wall built on top of it. Joist spans longer than 16 feet should be divided into shorter spans by a girder running down the middle.

Figure the size and lumber species for floor joists with the floor joist span tables on the opposite page and the instructions on this page. Verify the joist specifications with local code officials before installation. If you build with joists that don't meet code requirements, you might have to replace them before a building inspector will approve your addition.

Make sure the level of the new finished floor will match that of the existing floor, unless your plans call for different levels. If the existing floor is not level, decide which point to use as a reference for leveling the new floor. If the two floors will be connected only at a doorway, use the center of the doorway for the leveling point. If the two floors will be connected by two separate doors or by a wide opening, adjust the addition floor framing along its entire length to match the two floors.

Preparations for floor construction include arranging for the delivery of lumber and plywood. Have a bundle of shim shingles handy when you begin work on the floor.

Before you start work, be sure to address these two concerns:

■ If the foundation creates a crawl space with minimum access, and you plan to insulate either inside the walls or under the floor, install the insulation before you lay the subfloor. If there will be access to the new crawl space, plan your framing accordingly. Most additions provide access to the foundation area through a scuttle in a closet floor, an existing basement, or the foundation wall. If your access will be through the addition floor, frame the opening now.

■ If you have a large girder, such as a 4×12 or steel beam, arrange for enough help to lift it. A girder over a full basement might require one or more steel columns or Lally columns (steel pipe filled with concrete) for support. Ask your lumberyard what types are available and how long it will take to get one. If the post is not adjustable, be certain of your dimensions when you order it. You can substitute a pressure-treated 4×4.

DETERMINING JOIST SIZE WITH SPAN TABLES

The clear span of a joist (shown top right on the opposite page) is the horizontal distance between its supports. The allowable clear span depends on the dead load (weight of the floor itself), live load (weight of occupants and furnishings), joist size, plus the lumber species group and grade.

The tables on the opposite page make it easy to find the size joist you will need for your addition floor. If the addition is for a bedroom, use the table at the top; if it is for

CODE REQUIREMENTS

BEARING WALLS
A load-bearing wall must be supported on doubled joists, a solid beam, or separated double joists with blocking 4 feet on-center.

END SUPPORT
Ends of joists, beams, and girders must extend 1½ inches onto wood or metal or 3 inches onto masonry.

LATERAL RESTRAINT AT SUPPORTS
Joists must be laterally restrained at their supports. Use one of these methods:
■ install full-depth solid blocking
■ nail joists to a header, band, or rim joist
■ nail joists to adjacent stud

BRIDGING
Joists larger than 2×12 require bridging at least 10 feet on center. Use one of these:
■ full-depth solid blocking
■ diagonal wood or metal bridging
■ a 1×3 across the bottoms of the joists

DRILLING AND NOTCHING
Notches and holes must not occur in the middle one-third of a joist span.
■ Notches for ledgers at the ends cannot be deeper than ¼ of joist depth; other notches cannot exceed ⅙ of joist depth.
■ Holes cannot be within 2 inches of the joist top or bottom; hole diameter cannot be larger than ⅓ of joist depth.

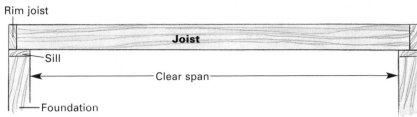

any other use, refer to the table at the bottom. Here are two examples:

EXAMPLE 1: You are adding a bedroom. The addition width is 16 feet, so the clear span between sills is 15 feet. Your local lumberyard has hem-fir (mixed species hemlock and fir) No. 1 framing lumber. If the joist spacing will be 16 inches on-center, what size joists should you buy?

To find the joist size, go to the Bedrooms table and find hem-fir, the second species group down on the left. Follow the 16-inch spacing row across to the right until you find a span greater than 15-0 (15 feet 0 inches) under No. 1. That is 17-8, under 2×10. The chart shows that you could use No. 2 2×10s for spans up to 16-10.

EXAMPLE 2: You are adding a family room.

The room is 20 feet wide, and a girder divides the span. The sills are 2×6 and the girder 6×12. With a joist spacing of 16 inches on-center, what is the required size of a No. 2 Southern yellow pine joist?

Since a family room is a habitable room other than a bedroom, use the table at the bottom. The clear span for your room is one-half of 18 feet 6 inches (20 feet minus 18 inches for the sills and girder), or 9 feet 3 inches. Follow the row for Southern pine, 16 inches on-center, to the right to find the smallest No. 2 joist that spans 9-3. The answer is a 2×6.

The joist span tables below are adapted from **The U.S. Span Book for Major Lumber Species,** *published by the Canadian Wood Council. The tables conform to most U.S. building codes and Federal Housing Authority (FHA) requirements.*

BEDROOMS (10 PSF DEAD LOAD, 30 PSF LIVE LOAD)

Allowable Clear Span of Joists, ft.–in.

Species Group	Spacing in. o.c.	Sel. Str.	2×6 No.1	No.2	No.3	Sel. Str.	2×8 No.1	No.2	No.3	Sel. Str.	2×10 No.1	No.2	No.3	Sel. Str.	2×12 No.1	No.2	No.3
Doug. Fir–Larch	12	12–6	12–0	11–10	9–8	16–6	15–10	15–7	12–4	21–0	20–3	19–10	15–0	25–7	24–8	23–0	17–5
	16	11–4	10–11	10–9	8–5	15–0	14–5	14–1	10–8	19–1	18–5	17–2	13–0	23–3	21–4	19–11	15–1
	24	9–11	9–7	9–1	6–10	13–1	12–4	11–6	8–8	16–8	15–0	14–1	10–7	20–3	17–5	16–3	12–4
Hem–Fir	12	11–10	11–7	11–0	9–8	15–7	15–3	14–6	12–4	19–10	19–5	18–6	15–0	24–2	23–7	22–6	17–5
	16	10–9	10–6	10–0	8–5	14–2	13–10	13–2	10–8	18–0	17–8	16–10	13–0	21–11	20–9	19–8	15–1
	24	9–4	9–2	8–9	6–10	12–4	12–0	11–4	8–8	15–9	14–8	13–10	10–7	19–2	17–0	16–1	12–4
Southern Pine	12	12–3	12–0	11–10	10–5	16–2	15–10	15–7	13–3	20–8	20–3	19–10	15–8	25–1	24–8	24–2	18–8
	16	11–2	10–11	10–9	9–0	14–8	14–5	14–2	11–6	18–9	18–5	18–0	13–7	22–10	22–5	21–1	16–2
	24	9–9	9–7	9–4	7–4	12–10	12–7	12–4	9–5	16–5	16–1	14–8	11–1	19–11	19–6	17–2	13–2

HABITABLE ROOMS EXCEPT BEDROOMS (10 PSF DEAD LOAD, 40 PSF LIVE LOAD)

Allowable Clear Span of Joists, ft.–in.

Species Group	Spacing in. o.c.	Sel. Str.	2×6 No.1	No.2	No.3	Sel. Str.	2×8 No.1	No.2	No.3	Sel. Str.	2×0 No.1	No.2	No.3	Sel. Str.	2×12 No.1	No.2	No.3
Doug. Fir–Larch	12	11–4	10–11	10–9	8–8	15–0	14–5	14–2	11–0	19–1	18–5	17–9	13–5	23–3	22–0	20–7	15–7
	16	10–4	9–11	9–9	7–6	13–7	13–1	12–7	9–6	17–4	16–5	15–5	11–8	21–1	19–1	17–10	13–6
	24	9–0	8–8	8–1	6–2	11–11	11–0	10–3	7–9	15–2	13–5	12–7	9–6	18–5	15–7	14–7	11–0
Hem–Fir	12	10–9	10–6	10–0	8–8	14–2	13–10	13–2	11–0	18–0	17–8	16–10	13–5	21–11	21–6	20–4	15–7
	16	9–9	9–6	9–1	7–6	12–10	12–7	12–0	9–6	16–5	16–0	15–2	11–8	19–11	18–7	17–7	13–6
	24	8–6	8–4	7–11	6–2	11–3	10–9	10–2	7–9	14–4	13–1	12–5	9–6	17–5	15–2	14–4	11–0
Southern Pine	12	11–2	10–11	10–9	9–4	14–8	14–5	14–2	11–11	18–9	18–5	18–0	14–0	22–10	22–5	21–9	16–8
	16	10–2	9–11	9–9	8–1	13–4	13–1	12–10	10–3	17–0	16–9	16–1	12–2	20–9	20–4	18–10	14–6
	24	8–10	8–8	8–6	6–7	11–8	11–5	11–0	8–5	14–11	14–7	13–1	9–11	18–1	17–5	15–5	11–10

FRAMING THE FLOOR

**ANATOMY OF A
WOOD-FRAME FLOOR**

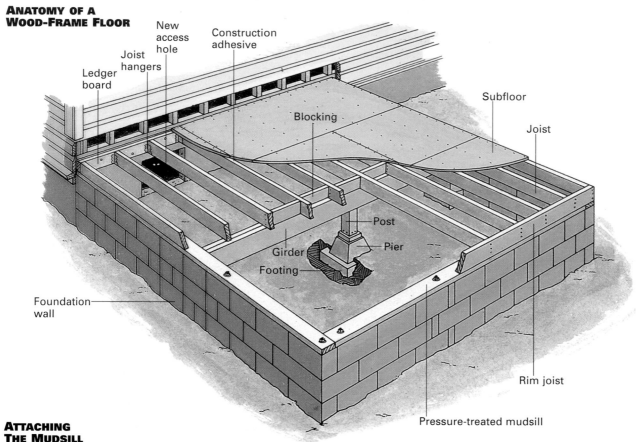

- New access hole
- Joist hangers
- Ledger board
- Construction adhesive
- Blocking
- Subfloor
- Joist
- Post
- Pier
- Girder
- Footing
- Foundation wall
- Rim joist
- Pressure-treated mudsill

**ATTACHING
THE MUDSILL**

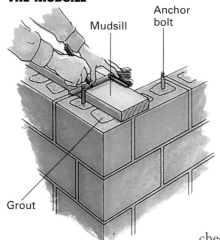

- Mudsill
- Anchor bolt
- Grout

SILLS

The sills, or mudsills—the bottommost pieces of wood in a building—are secured to the foundation by ½-inch anchor bolts. The floor framing is nailed to the sills, which are usually 2×6 or 2×8 pressure-treated pine.

To attach the sill, first check the plans to see whether it should lie flush with the outside edge of the foundation wall or should overhang the edge to allow for exterior foam foundation insulation. Next, mark the locations of the anchor bolts by laying the sill next to the bolts. Drill ¾-inch-diameter holes at the marks.

If the flatness of the top of the foundation varies by more than ¼ inch, mix a small batch of mortar and fill the low spots before laying the sill.

For basements or heated crawl spaces, install a layer of sill seal, a compressible, closed-cell plastic foam insulation, under the sill to stop air infiltration.

In some areas, a metal termite shield must also be installed under the sill. Roll 10-inch-wide aluminum flashing out over the foundation so it laps 2 inches over the outside edge; push it down over the bolts as you draw it tight. Cut bolt holes with a utility knife. Cover the aluminum with roofing cement—especially around the bolt holes and at any splices— just before installing the sill.

Then set the sill in place. Using a taut chalk line as a guide, keep the sill straight as you tighten the bolts.

GIRDERS

A girder can be a solid beam or it can be built from 2× lumber. Building codes usually require at least 3 inches of bearing surface under each end of a girder. If the girder is not pressure-treated, line the foundation pockets with aluminum flashing or asphalt roofing to prevent direct contact with the concrete. Shim or notch the girder to bring its edge flush with the sill.

If the girder rests on a steel column, loosely bolt it to the flange, then level it before tightening the bolts. Shim as needed.

If wood posts support the girder, connect the girder to the posts with metal post caps, using 16d joist hanger nails.

JOISTS

Joists are normally spaced 16 inches on center, but they can also be spaced 12 or 24 inches on center, depending on the subfloor.

Select three straight joists for the three outside rim joists and nail the ends together. This is your last chance to make the floor square, so measure the two diagonals and adjust the joists until the diagonals are equal. Toenail the rim joists to the sills with 8d galvanized nails.

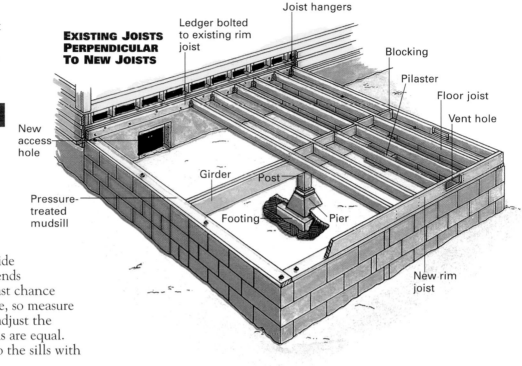

EXISTING JOISTS PARALLEL TO NEW JOISTS

If the new joists run perpendicular to the existing foundation wall and the existing joists, bolt a new 2× ledger to the rim joist and attach the joists to it with joist hangers.

If, instead, the new joists run perpendicular to the common foundation wall and parallel to the existing joists, remove the old rim joist. Overlap the new joists beside the old, shim the new joists so the tops are flush, and nail them together with 16d nails staggered every 16 inches. Install blocking between them along the top of the original sill.

Mark the locations of the floor joists on the rim joists and girder, starting from the same end. Face-nail each joist to the rim joist with three or four 16d galvanized common nails and toenail it to the sill below with three 8d nails. Install all joists with their crowns, or convex-curved edges, up. Install blocking between the joists over the girder and at the midpoint of any span longer than 8 feet. If the joists are attached to the girder with joist hangers, nail the hangers to the joist ends first, then to the girder, to ensure that the tops will be flush. Double up joists that fall under interior walls.

FLOOR STEPPED OVER GIRDER

STAIRS AND SUBFLOORING

FRAMING AND BUILDING STAIRS

You'll need stairs to provide access to a basement or second floor directly from your addition. Rough-in the stairs as early as possible to make construction easier.

CALCULATING STAIR DIMENSIONS: Measure the vertical distance from finish floor to finish floor (108 inches, for our example). Divide this distance by 7.5 inches, the standard riser height. Round the answer up to the next whole number, and divide the actual measurement by that number to find the height of each riser. To determine tread width, subtract the riser height from $17\frac{1}{2}$ inches.

RISER EXAMPLE:
108 inches / 7.5 inches = 14.4 steps (15)
108 inches / 15 steps = $7\frac{3}{16}$ inches per step

TREAD EXAMPLE:
$17\frac{1}{2}$ inches − $7\frac{3}{16}$ inches = $10\frac{5}{16}$ inches

FRAMING THE STAIRWELL: Frame the rough opening for the stairs with headers and trimmer joists as shown below left.

INSTALLING THE STAIRS: Select three straight 2×12s. Set a framing square so the short leg intersects the top edge of the first 2×12 at the riser dimension and the long leg at the tread dimension. Scribe the outline on the stringer.

Slide the square along the 2×12 until it meets the first riser, and scribe. Mark all steps this way. Cut out the steps. To make the bottom step the same height as the others, trim the bottom of the stringer by the thickness of a tread. Then cut a notch for the 2×4 cleat. Check the stringer for fit in the

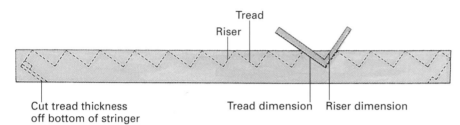

Tread
Riser

Cut tread thickness off bottom of stringer

Tread dimension   Riser dimension

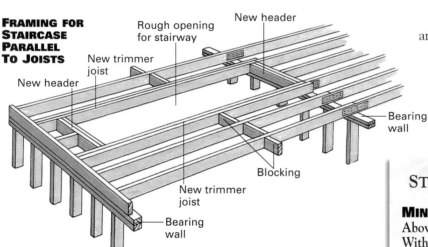

FRAMING FOR STAIRCASE PARALLEL TO JOISTS

New header
Rough opening for stairway
New header
New trimmer joist
New trimmer joist
New header
Blocking
Bearing wall
Bearing wall

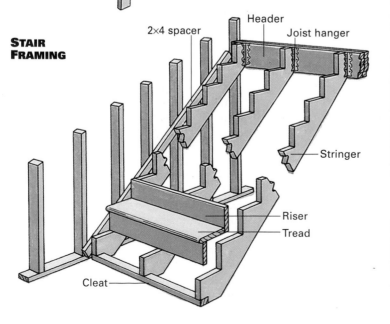

STAIR FRAMING

2×4 spacer
Header
Joist hanger
Stringer
Riser
Tread
Cleat

STAIR CODE REQUIREMENTS

MINIMUM WIDTH
Above handrail: 36 inches
With one handrail: 32 inches
Between two handrails: 28 inches

HEADROOM
At least 80 inches at all points

RISERS AND TREADS
Maximum riser height: $7\frac{3}{4}$ inches
Maximum riser variation: $\frac{3}{8}$ inch
Minimum tread, nose to nose: 10 inches

HANDRAILS
Required with three or more risers
Height above tread nosing: 30–38 inches
Minimum distance from wall: $1\frac{1}{2}$ inches

GUARDRAILS
Required more than 30 inches above floor
Minimum rail height: 36 inches
Must block 4-inch-diameter sphere

THE SUBFLOOR
APA RECOMMENDED SUBFLOOR

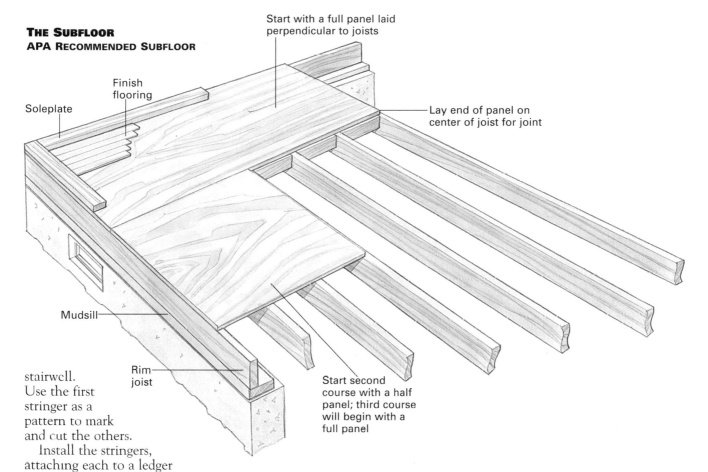

Start with a full panel laid perpendicular to joists

Lay end of panel on center of joist for joint

Soleplate

Finish flooring

Mudsill

Rim joist

Start second course with a half panel; third course will begin with a full panel

stairwell. Use the first stringer as a pattern to mark and cut the others.

Install the stringers, attaching each to a ledger or joist hangers at the top and a cleat at the bottom. For a stringer against a wall, nail a 2×4 spacer between the studs and the stringer to allow for wallboard and finish trim.

Cut risers from 1× lumber. Cut the treads from special tread stock with a rounded nose. Rip it to a width equal to the tread dimension plus the tread thickness (usually 1¼ inches). If the stairs are to be carpeted, you can use ¾- and 1-inch plywood for risers and treads.

Attach risers and treads with construction adhesive and ringshank nails. Face-nail both into the stringers, and drive nails from the backs of the risers into the treads.

The handrail can be attached to the wall or supported by balusters and newel posts for open stairways. Allow at least 1½ inches between the handrail and a wall.

THE SUBFLOOR

Subfloors are usually ⅝- or ¾-inch plywood or structural oriented-strand board (OSB). Sheathing-grade plywood is acceptable if the finish floor will be wood or heavy carpet; resilient sheet flooring or other thin material will require a solid-core underlayment, such as ⁵⁄₃₂-inch lauan plywood.

Unless you are matching existing ⅝-inch plywood in the original house, install ¾-inch plywood for a stronger floor in your addition,

even though ⅝-inch plywood is allowed by most codes.

Smooth plywood and OSB panels labeled APA Rated Sturdifloor are more expensive but are suitable for any kind of finish floor except tile. Tile should have an additional layer of ½-inch grade C-C plugged tongue-and-groove plywood glued over the subfloor to prevent flexing.

INSTALLING SUBFLOORING: Install plywood panels with the long dimension perpendicular to the joists. Start by snapping a chalk line 4 feet from the outside edge of the rim joist. Install a full panel first.

To prevent the floor from squeaking, apply construction adhesive to the top edges of the joists with a caulking gun just before laying each panel. Nail the panels with 6d ringshank nails every 6 inches around the edges and every 12 inches on the interior.

Leave space between the panels at the joints to prevent buckling if the floor gets wet. The manufacturer might specify a gap amount; otherwise, carpenters sometimes use a nickel as a spacer. Under sheet vinyl, underlayment should have a gap of ¹⁄₃₂ inch.

After finishing the first row of panels, cut a full panel in half, and stagger the panel joints 4 feet on the remaining rows. All joints must be on joists.

WALLS

WALL HEIGHT

Framing addition walls is the same as framing any other wall, except that you may have to match the height of nonstandard existing house walls. For the ceilings in the main house to flow continuously into the addition, you must figure the framing height and finish ceiling thicknesses closely. If there are framed doorways between the old and new areas, a ceiling height difference of a few inches will not be apparent.

CODE REQUIREMENTS

TOP PLATES

Top plates must be doubled with overlapping corners. Joints must overlap by at least 48 inches.

JOIST AND RAFTER SUPPORT

Joists and rafters must be within 5 inches of a bearing stud if the joists or rafters are spaced more than 16 inches on center and the bearing studs are spaced 24 inches on center, except in the following cases:
■ top plates are double 2×6s or 3×4s
■ top plates are tripled
■ solid blocking reinforces the top plate

NONBEARING PARTITIONS

Interior nonbearing partitions may be built with a single top plate. Minimum stud requirements are either of the following:
■ 2×3 studs spaced 24 inches on center
■ 2×4 flat studs spaced 16 inches on center

NOTCHING

Notches in load-bearing studs must not exceed 25 percent of stud width; in nonbearing studs, 40 percent of width.

HOLES

The diameter of a hole must not exceed 40 percent of stud width (60 percent for double studs), if the hole is ⅝ inch or more from edge. When drilling or notching a top plate more than 50 percent of its width, reinforce it with 24-gauge steel angle.

FIRESTOPPING

Required Firestopping locations:
■ tops and bottoms of walls
■ intersections of walls and ceilings
■ tops and bottoms of stair stringers
■ openings in floors and ceilings

WALL THICKNESS

Exterior walls are usually framed with either 2×4 studs 16 inches on-center, or 2×6 studs 24 inches on-center. The cost of either framing is about the same. Factors to consider include:
■ Thicker insulation in the 2×6 wall reduces heat loss through the wall by about one-third.
■ Most people like the deeper-set windows of the thicker wall.
■ The thicker wall requires extension jambs for windows, at additional cost.

Before you decide, check with local code officials. Your locality may have an energy code which requires the higher R-value of the 2×6 wall.

VERIFY YOUR PLANS

You can't plan too much before you actually start framing. As soon as the subfloor is finished, snap chalk lines on it to show the locations of all walls and windows. Spend some time walking around on it and try to imagine how the finished space will feel, how the windows will look, what scenes will be framed by the windows when you sit and when you stand, and how the doorways will work. Don't hesitate to change the sizes and locations of walls, doorways, and windows before placing your final order for materials.

Moving a doorway or window a few inches at this point is much easier than moving it after it has been framed. You can usually move walls, doors, and windows a few inches without concern. But major plan changes, such as enlarging the glazed area or raising the ceiling height, should be approved by local code officials.

DOUBLE-CHECK ROUGH OPENINGS

The most common framing errors are due to having the wrong rough-opening dimensions for windows and doors. The rough opening is the width and height of the opening in the wall framing members—usually it is about ½ inch larger than the jamb size. Make sure you have the correct rough-opening sizes for your windows and doors, taken from the current manufacturer's catalog. It's better to have your windows and doors on site so you can measure them before starting to frame the walls.

PREPARING THE COMMON WALL

If you will be removing the common wall between the house and the addition or creating a large opening in it, determine whether it should be done now or if it can be postponed until you finish the shell. Do it now if the opening is wider than 6 feet and the wall supports the house roof or second floor. To see how, turn to Creating a Large Opening on page 70.

Start by preparing the house wall where the addition walls will attach. Remove siding and trim that would interfere with a direct connection between existing and new framing. If the new wall intersects the house between two studs, install horizontal blocking between the studs every 2 feet, or add studs to the house wall to create a three-stud corner at the intersection.

Construct each new wall flat on the subfloor and raise it into place, starting with the walls that connect to the house. The

TYPICAL STUD WALL

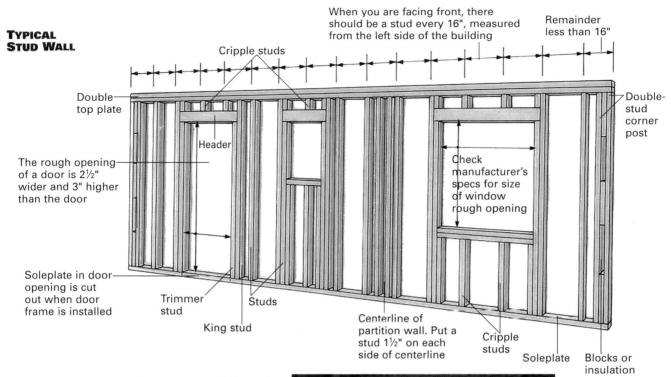

remaining exterior wall comes next, followed by interior partition walls.

Arrange for people to help you raise long walls. Have at least one person for every 10 feet of single-story wall or one person for every 4 feet of two-story wall.

Have at least one safe, sturdy stepladder or ladder tall enough for nailing the cap plates.

COMPONENTS

PLATES: The soleplate and top plate tie the wall together and provide nailing or top and bottom of sheathing and drywall.

STUDS: These vertical members support the load of the roof, the ceiling, or the floor above. They carry sheathing, siding, and drywall. They are spaced either 16 inches (2×4 wall) or 24 inches (2×6 wall) on-center so that they fall directly under ceiling joists and rafters, as well as at the edges of sheathing and drywall panels.

HEADERS: These horizontal beams span door and window openings and rest on the trimmer studs.

TRIMMER STUDS: These short studs set the height of openings.

KING STUDS: These are the tall studs outside wall openings. The trimmers fasten to them.

CRIPPLE STUDS: These short studs typically support windowsills.

CORNER POST: This arrangement of studs provides nailing for drywall on inside corners.

HEADER SPANS

The headers support the ceiling and roof loads above windows and doors. Use the table below to find the proper headers.

EXAMPLE: Your addition is 20 feet wide and the code specifies a snow load of 40 pounds per square foot (psf). What are your options for headers over a window with a rough opening of 6 feet 3 inches?

To find the answer, look under the 40 psf snow load column for the building width of 20 feet. The column (third from right) shows the smallest headers to span at least 6–3 are two 2×10s or three 2×8s.

EXTERIOR WALL HEADERS SUPPORTING ROOF AND CEILING

| Snow Load | 20 psf | | | 30 psf | | | 40 psf | | |
| | Building Width, ft. | | | Building Width, ft. | | | Building Width, ft. | | |
Header	20	28	36	20	28	36	20	28	36
2–2×4	3–6	3–2	2–10	3–3	2–10	2–7	3–0	2–7	2–4
2–2×6	5–5	4–8	4–2	4–10	4–2	3–9	4–5	3–10	3–5
2–2×8	6–10	5–11	5–4	6–2	5–4	4–9	5–7	4–10	4–4
2–2×10	8–5	7–3	6–6	7–6	6–6	5–10	6–10	5–11	5–4
2–2×12	9–9	8–5	7–6	8–8	7–6	6–9	7–11	6–10	6–2
3–2×8	8–4	7–5	6–8	7–8	6–8	5–11	7–0	6–1	5–5
3–2×10	10–6	9–1	8–2	9–5	8–2	7–3	8–7	7–5	6–8
3–2×12	12–2	10–7	9–5	10–11	9–5	8–5	9–11	8–7	7–8
4–2×8	9–2	8–4	7–8	8–6	7–8	6–11	8–0	7–0	6–3
4–2×10	11–8	10–6	9–5	10–10	9–5	8–5	9–11	8–7	7–8
4–2×12	14–1	12–2	10–11	12–7	10–11	9–9	11–6	9–11	8–11

BUILDING WALLS

**INSTALLING
A VERTICAL
3-STUD**

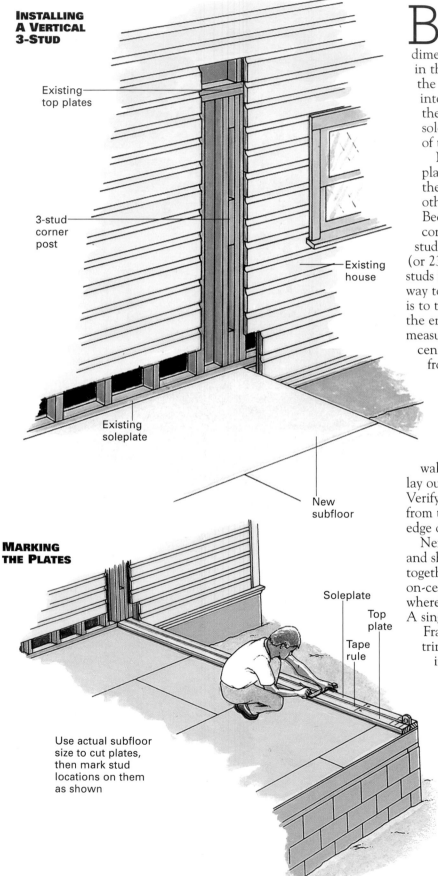

Existing
top plates

3-stud
corner
post

Existing
house

Existing
soleplate

New
subfloor

**MARKING
THE PLATES**

Soleplate

Top
plate

Tape
rule

Use actual subfloor
size to cut plates,
then mark stud
locations on them
as shown

B egin wall construction by cutting the soleplate and one of the top plates to length. Use the actual subfloor dimension if it's different from the dimension in the plan. (It should be within ¼ inch.) If the house framing at the point of intersection is not perfectly plumb, adjust the length of the top plate so the top and soleplates will be plumb at the other corner of the wall.

Next, mark the stud locations on the plates. To ensure that the layout starts from the same end, lay the plates beside each other and mark both at the same time. Because the measurements start at the corner of the wall instead of the center of a stud, the mark for the first stud will be 15¼ (or 23¼) inches from the end. The rest of the studs fall 16 (or 24) inches on-center. A good way to make this measurement less confusing is to tack a ¾-inch-thick scrap of wood onto the end of the plates and hook the tape measure over it. This automatically places the center of the first stud the correct distance from the end.

Determine the locations of doors and windows. Mark the rough-opening width on the plates for the trimmer studs, then mark the king studs next to them.

You should also note where interior walls will intersect the exterior wall, and lay out stud locations for the intersections. Verify whether the measurements you take from the plan refer to the center or to an edge of these intersections.

Next, build up corner posts from two studs and short blocking, face-nailing them together with 16-penny (16d) nails, 16 inches on-center. You will not need full corner posts where a wall is nailed into another wall. A single stud will suffice there.

Frame each opening with a header, trimmer studs, king studs, and a sill, if needed. The nailing sequence is:

1. For windows only—face-nail the rough sill between two trimmer studs with two 16d nails at each end. For a double sill, nail the sill 1½ inches lower than the rough opening to allow for the top sill.

2. Cut the header to length (rough-opening dimension plus 3 inches) and position it at the top of the trimmer studs.

3. Lay the king studs in place next to the trimmer studs, and face-nail them to the header with at least four 16d nails at each end.

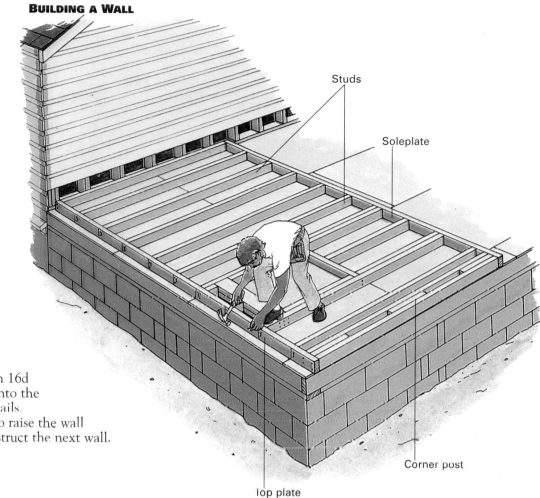

BUILDING A WALL

4. Face-nail both pairs of king and trimmer studs together with 16d nails, 24 inches on-center.

Next, face-nail the completed corner and all opening assemblies to the soleplate and top plate with two 16d nails at both ends of each stud. Face-nail all remaining studs to the plates with pairs of 16d nails.

The last step is to cut and install any cripple studs, face-nailing into the rough windowsill with 16d nails and toenailing into the header with four 8d nails.

You're now ready to raise the wall to make room to construct the next wall.

Studs

Soleplate

Corner post

Top plate

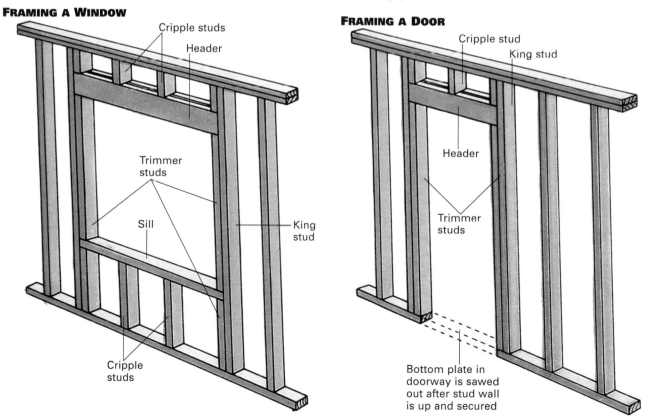

FRAMING A WINDOW

Cripple studs

Header

Trimmer studs

Sill

King stud

Cripple studs

FRAMING A DOOR

Cripple stud

King stud

Header

Trimmer studs

Bottom plate in doorway is sawed out after stud wall is up and secured

RAISING A WALL

Snap a chalk line 3½ inches inside the edge of the subfloor (5½ inches for 2×6 walls) to mark the edge of the wall.

As a safety precaution, nail vertical blocks to the outside of the rim joist to keep the base of the wall from sliding off as you lift it. Then lift the wall into place.

Nail through the soleplate and subfloor into the joists with 16d nails. Using a 4-foot level, plumb the wall and nail it to the house framing. Next, plumb the wall at the corner, and brace it temporarily as shown in the illustration below.

When all of the walls are in place, install the cap plates, overlapping at all corners.

If you built a long wall in two sections, make sure the cap plate extends at least 4 feet beyond the joint in both directions.

You can install permanent bracing now or after the roof is on. Covering the wall with plywood, oriented-strand board, or any other structural sheathing satisfies the code requirement for bracing.

ALIGNING AND BRACING THE WALL

Use a long level to align the new stud wall vertically and nail it to the existing house

Chalk line 3½" inside edge of subfloor

Brace holds walls until cap plates are installed

TYING A WALL TO THE OLD ROOF

Before framing a second-story wall to butt against an existing roof, cut the existing roofing, roof sheathing, and any overhanging structure back so that it aligns with the edge of the new floor framing. Then, if the gable-end wall isn't required to support the end rafter (most aren't), remove it, too.

Frame and raise the new second-floor wall against the old roof. At the same time, frame in a doorway (it doesn't have to be full-height) for access to the attic.

Cut a pair of 2×4 or 2×6 rafters and, holding them up against the existing roof sheathing inside the attic, nail them to the new stud wall from the attic side. Nail the

sheathing to the new rafters, either from above or with angle-framing clips from below.

Cut and install angled 2× blocking between the studs to follow the roofline, just above the plane of the roofing. Install plywood sheathing on the exterior wall, butting the bottom against the roof sheathing.

Reshingle over the strip of bare roof sheathing before installing the final siding. Slip step flashing against the wall sheathing at each course of roofing shingles (see Step Flashing on page 63.

When you install the siding, leave 1 inch of clearance between the bottom of the siding and the roofing.

TYING NEW WALLS TO OLD ROOF

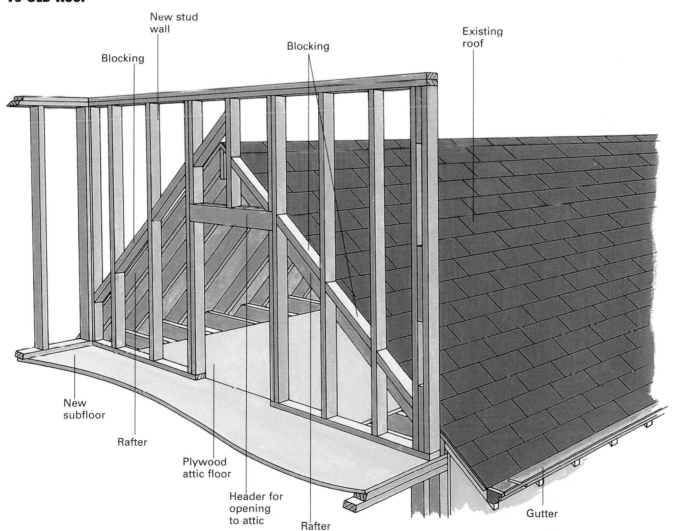

DETERMINING THE SLOPE OF THE ROOF

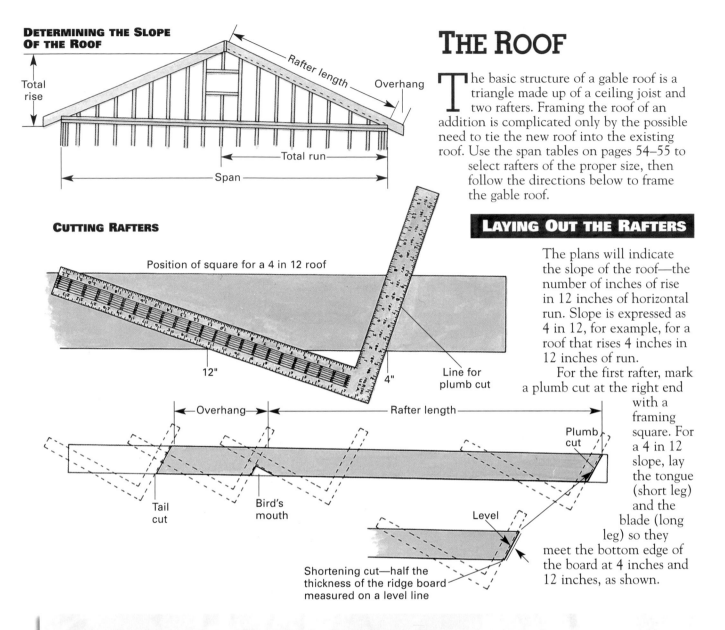

Total rise

Rafter length

Overhang

Total run

Span

CUTTING RAFTERS

Position of square for a 4 in 12 roof

12"

4"

Line for plumb cut

Overhang

Rafter length

Plumb cut

Tail cut

Bird's mouth

Level

Shortening cut—half the thickness of the ridge board measured on a level line

THE ROOF

The basic structure of a gable roof is a triangle made up of a ceiling joist and two rafters. Framing the roof of an addition is complicated only by the possible need to tie the new roof into the existing roof. Use the span tables on pages 54–55 to select rafters of the proper size, then follow the directions below to frame the gable roof.

LAYING OUT THE RAFTERS

The plans will indicate the slope of the roof—the number of inches of rise in 12 inches of horizontal run. Slope is expressed as 4 in 12, for example, for a roof that rises 4 inches in 12 inches of run.

For the first rafter, mark a plumb cut at the right end with a framing square. For a 4 in 12 slope, lay the tongue (short leg) and the blade (long leg) so they meet the bottom edge of the board at 4 inches and 12 inches, as shown.

CODE REQUIREMENTS

ROOF FRAMING:
■ Rafters parallel to joists must be tied to them.
■ Rafters not parallel to joists must have rafter ties.
■ Place rafter ties as close as possible to the top plate.
■ Space rafter ties no more than 4 feet apart.
■ Make the ridge board at least ¾ inch thick and as wide as the rafter ends.
■ Tie or gusset rafter tops to the ridge board.
■ Make valley and hip rafters at least 1½ inches thick, as wide as the ends.

CEILING JOISTS
Lap ceiling joists at least 3 inches or tie them together to resist the thrust of the rafters.

END BEARING
Rafter and ceiling joists must bear on their supports by at least 1½ inches on wood or metal or 3 inches on masonry.

CUTTING/NOTCHING
Notches in rafters and ceiling joists must not exceed these limits:

■ ¼ depth at ends
■ ⅙ depth in top or bottom, not in the middle ⅓ of the member
■ ⅓ depth in top when the notch is placed less than the member's depth horizontally from support

HOLES
Holes bored in rafters and ceiling joists must not be within 2 inches of the top or bottom edge. The hole's diameter cannot be more than ⅓ of the depth of the joist or rafter.

BRIDGING
Rafters with a depth-to-thickness ratio greater than 6-1 (larger than 2×12, for example) require bridging at least every 10 feet on-center. Use any of these:
■ full-depth solid blocking
■ diagonal wood or metal
■ 1×3 strip at bottom

WIND
Roofs subject to wind uplift of 20 psf or more must have truss or rafter ties effectively connected to the foundation.

To determine the length of the rafter, refer to the numbers stamped on the longer blade of the square. The 12.65 under the 4-inch mark means that for every foot of horizontal run, rafter length will be 12.65 inches. If the run were 8 feet (half of a total span of 16 feet), the rafter length for a 4-in-12 roof would be 101.2 inches (8×12.65), or 8 feet 5¼ inches. Measure the rafter length from the plumb cut, and mark the top edge of the board. Set the square at 4 in 12 again, and scribe a plumb line there.

Then slide the square, still in its 4-in-12 position, back toward the original plumb cut until it creates a line for the seat of the bird's mouth exactly the width of the 2×4 cap plate (3½ inches).

Next, mark the tail cut by sliding the square beyond the bird's mouth by the length of the overhang. Finally, go back to your first mark and move the plumb cut toward the bird's mouth by half the thickness of the ridge board (⅜ inch for a ¾-inch ridge board).

Cut the first pair of rafters. Test their fit by placing the pair in position with a scrap of ridge board between them at the peak. Adjust as necessary. Once they have been adjusted to fit well, use the adjusted rafter as a pattern for the remaining rafters. After you have cut all of the rafters, set them aside until you have installed the ceiling joists.

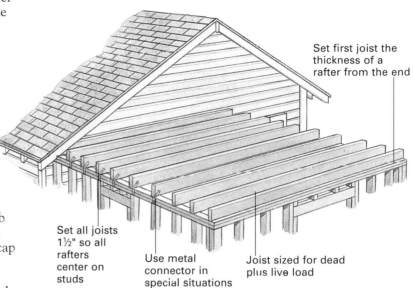

Set first joist the thickness of a rafter from the end

Set all joists 1½" so all rafters center on studs

Use metal connector in special situations

Joist sized for dead plus live load

CEILING JOISTS

SELECTION: If the space under the rafters will be occupied, the ceiling joists will also be floor joists, so use the floor-joist span tables on page 41 to select ceiling joists. Otherwise, use the table below.

INSTALLATION: Mark the locations of the rafter seats on the cap plates. The outside of the first rafter should be flush with the outside of the gable wall. Set the first ceiling joist in from the wall to make room for the gable-end studs and to provide a nailing surface for the finish ceiling.

Toenail the ceiling joists to the cap plates next to the rafter locations. The ceiling joists will be nailed to the rafters over the cap plates in order to complete the roof triangle and prevent the walls from spreading under the roof load. Trim the top corners of the joists flush with the rafter slope. Where earthquakes or high winds are a factor, attach the joists with metal framing clips. This framework can be a convenient scaffold during installation of the rafters.

CEILING JOISTS WITH LIMITED ATTIC STORAGE
(10 PSF DEAD LOAD, 20 PSF LIVE LOAD)

Allowable Clear Span of Joists, ft.–in.

Species Group	Spacing in. o.c.	2×4 Sel. Str.	No.1	No.2	No.3	2×6 Sel. Str.	No.1	No.2	No.3	2×8 Sel. Str.	No.1	No.2	No.3
Douglas	12	10–5	10–0	9–10	7–8	16–4	15–9	14–10	11–2	21–7	20–1	18–9	14–2
Fir–	16	9–6	9–1	8–9	6–8	14–11	13–9	12–10	9–8	19–7	17–5	16–3	12–4
Larch	24	8–3	7–8	7–2	5–5	13–0	11–2	10–6	7–11	17–1	14–2	13–3	10–0
Hem–Fir	12	9–10	9–8	9–2	7–8	15–6	15–2	14–5	11–2	20–5	19–7	18–6	14–2
	16	8–11	8–9	8–4	6–8	14–1	13–5	12–8	9–8	18–6	16–11	16–0	12–4
	24	7–10	7–6	7–1	5–5	12–3	10–11	10–4	7–11	16–2	13–10	13–1	10–0
Southern	12	10–3	10–0	9–10	8–2	16–1	15–9	15–6	12–0	21–2	20–10	20–1	15–4
Pine	16	9–4	9–1	8–11	7–1	14–7	14–4	13–6	10–5	19–3	18–11	17–5	13–3
	24	8–1	8–0	7–8	5–9	12–9	12–6	11–0	8–6	16–10	15–10	14–2	10–10

RAFTER SPAN TABLES

The span table below can be used to specify rafters for roofs that will be covered with heavy roofing, such as tile and slate. The assumed total weight of the structure plus roofing for such a roof is 20 pounds per square foot (psf). The table on the opposite page is for roofs covered with light roofing, such as asphalt roofing, with an assumed total weight of 10 psf.

Before using the tables, note the definition of rafter clear span.

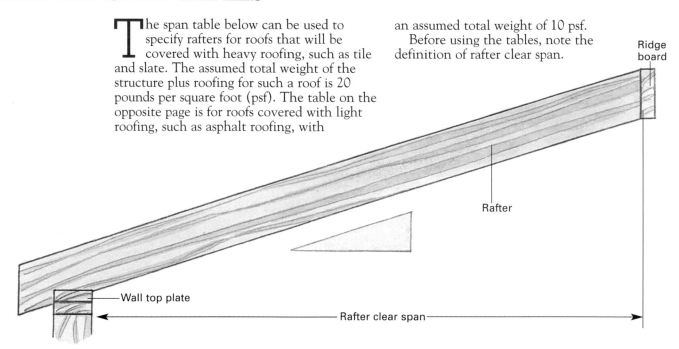

Ridge board

Rafter

Wall top plate

Rafter clear span

HEAVY ROOFING, NO CEILING (20 PSF DEAD LOAD)

Allowable Clear Span of Rafters, ft.–in.

Species Group	Spacing in. o.c.	2×4 Sel. Str.	No.1	No.2	No.3	2×6 Sel. Str.	No.1	No.2	No.3	2×8 Sel. Str.	No.1	No.2	No.3	2×10 Sel. Str.	No.1	No.2	No.3
20 PSF SNOW LOAD																	
Douglas	12	11–6	10–1	9–5	7–1	17–9	14–9	13–9	10–5	22–5	18–8	17–5	13–2	27–5	22–9	21–4	16–1
Fir–	16	10–5	8–9	8–2	6–2	15–4	12–9	11–11	9–0	19–5	16–2	15–1	11–5	23–9	19–9	18–5	13–11
Larch	24	8–7	7–1	6–8	5–0	12–6	10–5	9–9	7–4	15–10	13–2	12–4	9–4	19–5	16–1	15–1	11–5
Hem–Fir	12	10–10	9–10	9–3	7–1	17–0	14–4	13–7	10–5	22–1	18–2	17–2	13–2	26–11	22–2	21–0	16–1
	16	9–10	8–6	8–0	6–2	15–1	12–5	11–9	9–0	19–1	15–9	14–11	11–5	23–4	19–3	18–2	13–11
	24	8–5	6–11	6–7	5–0	12–4	10–2	9–7	7–4	15–7	12–10	12–2	9–4	19–1	15–8	14–10	11–5
Southern	12	11–3	11–1	10–1	7–7	17–8	16–7	14–5	11–2	23–4	20–10	18–8	14–3	29–9	24–9	22–3	16–10
Pine	16	10–3	9–8	8–9	6–7	16–1	14–4	12–6	9–8	21–2	18–1	16–2	12–4	26–11	21–5	19–3	14–7
	24	8–11	7–11	7–1	5–4	14–1	11–9	10–2	7–11	18–3	14–9	13–2	10–1	22–0	17–6	15–9	11–11
30 PSF SNOW LOAD																	
Douglas	12	10–0	9–0	8–5	6–4	15–9	13–2	12–4	9–4	20–1	16–8	15–7	11–9	24–6	20–4	19–1	14–5
Fir–	16	9–1	7–10	7–3	5–6	13–9	11–5	10–8	8–1	17–5	14–5	13–6	10–3	21–3	17–8	16–6	12–6
Larch	24	7–8	6–4	4–11	4–6	11–3	9–4	8–9	6–7	14–2	11–9	11–0	8–4	17–4	14–5	13–6	10–2
Hem–Fir	12	9–6	8–9	8–4	6–4	14–10	12–10	12–2	9–4	19–7	16–3	15–4	11–9	24–1	19–10	18–9	14–5
	16	8–7	7–7	7–2	5–6	13–6	11–1	10–6	8–1	17–1	14–1	13–4	10–3	20–10	17–2	16–3	12–6
	24	7–6	6–2	5–10	4–6	11–0	9–1	8–7	6–7	13–11	11–6	10–10	8–4	17–1	14–0	13–3	10–2
Southern	12	9–10	9–8	9–0	6–9	15–6	14–10	12–11	10–0	20–5	18–8	16–8	12–9	26–0	22–2	19–11	15–1
Pine	16	8–11	8–8	7–10	5–10	14–1	12–10	11–2	8–8	18–6	16–2	14–5	11–0	23–8	19–2	17–3	13–0
	24	7–10	7–1	6–4	4–9	12–3	10–6	9–2	7–1	16–2	13–2	11–9	9–0	19–8	15–8	14–1	10–8

As shown in the illustration, it is the horizontal distance between supports, not the length of the rafter.

EXAMPLE: A 20-foot-wide building has 2×6 walls, is roofed with asphalt shingles, and is in an area where a 30 psf snow load can be expected. The gable rafters are No. 1 Douglas fir-larch, placed 24 inches on-center. What size rafter meets the specifications?

Refer to the chart for light roofing. The rafter clear span is 9 feet 6⅛ inches (10 feet-5½ inches − ⅜ inch). Under 30 psf snow load, read across the line for Douglas fir-larch, 24-inch spacing, to find a 10-5 span, a 2×6.

LIGHT ROOFING, NO CEILING (10 PSF DEAD LOAD)

Allowable Clear Span of Rafters, ft.–in.

Species Group	Spacing in. o.c.	2×4				2×6				2×8				2×10			
		Sel. Str.	No.1	No.2	No.3	Sel. Str.	No.1	No.2	No.3	Sel. Str.	No.1	No.2	No.3	Sel. Str.	No.1	No.2	No.3
20 PSF SNOW LOAD																	
Douglas	12	11–6	11–1	10–10	8–3	18–0	17–0	15–11	12–0	23–9	21–6	20–2	15–3	30–4	26–4	24–7	18–7
Fir–	16	10–5	10–0	9–5	7–1	16–4	14–9	13–9	10–5	21–7	18–8	17–5	13–2	27–5	22–9	21–4	16–1
Larch	24	9–1	8–3	7–8	5–10	14–4	12–0	11–3	8–6	18–4	15–3	14–3	10–9	22–5	18–7	17–5	13–2
Hem–Fir	12	10–10	10–7	10–1	8–3	17–0	16–7	15–8	12–0	22–5	21–0	19–10	15–3	28–7	25–8	24–3	18–7
	16	9–10	9–8	9–2	7–1	15–6	14–4	13–7	10–5	20–5	18–2	17–2	13–2	26–0	22–2	21–0	16–1
	24	8–7	8–0	7–7	5–10	13–6	11–9	11–1	8–6	17–10	14–10	14–0	10–9	22–0	18–1	17–2	13–2
Southern	12	11–3	11–1	10–10	8–9	17–8	17–4	16–8	12–11	23–4	22–11	21–6	16–5	29–9	28–7	25–8	19–5
Pine	16	10–3	10–0	9–10	7–7	16–1	15–9	14–5	11–2	21–2	20–10	18–8	14–3	27–1	24–9	22–3	16–10
	24	8–11	8–9	8–3	6–2	14–1	13–6	11–9	9–2	18–6	17–0	15–3	11–8	23–8	20–3	18–2	13–9
30 PSF SNOW LOAD																	
Douglas	12	10–0	9–8	9–5	7–1	15–9	14–9	13–9	10–5	20–9	18–8	17–5	13–2	26–6	22–9	21–4	16–1
Fir-	16	9–1	8–9	8–2	6–2	14–4	12–9	11–11	9–0	18–10	16–2	15–1	11–5	23–9	19–9	18–5	13–11
Larch	24	7–11	7–1	6–8	5–0	12–6	10–5	9–9	7–4	15–10	13–2	12–4	9–4	19–5	16–1	15–1	11–5
Hem-Fir	12	9–6	9–3	8–10	7–1	14–10	14–4	13–7	10–5	19–7	18–2	17–2	13–2	25–0	22–2	21–0	16–1
	16	8–7	8–5	8–0	6–2	13–6	12–5	11–9	9–0	17–10	15–9	14–11	11–5	22–9	19–3	18–2	13–11
	24	7–6	6–11	6–7	5–0	11–10	10–2	9–7	7–4	15–7	12–10	12–2	9–4	19–1	15–8	14–10	11–5
Southern	12	9–10	9–8	9–6	7–7	15–6	15–2	14–5	11–2	20–5	20–0	18–8	14–3	26–0	24–9	22–3	16–10
Pine	16	8–11	8–9	8–7	6–7	14–1	13–9	12–6	9–8	18–6	18–1	16–2	12–4	23–8	21–5	19–3	14–7
	24	7–10	7–8	7–1	5–4	12–3	11–9	10–2	7–11	16–2	14–9	13–2	10–1	20–8	17–6	15–9	11–11
40 PSF SNOW LOAD																	
Douglas	12	13–0	12–6	12–3	9–4	17–2	16–6	15–7	11–9	21–10	20–4	19–1	14–5	26–7	23–7	22–1	16–8
Fir–	16	11–10	11–5	10–8	8–1	15–7	14–5	13–6	10–3	19–10	17–8	16–6	12–6	24–2	20–5	19–2	14–6
Larch	24	10–4	9–4	8–9	6–7	13–7	11–9	11–0	8–4	17–4	14–5	13–6	10–2	20–1	16–8	15–7	11–10
Hem–Fir	12	12–3	12–0	11–5	9–4	16–2	15–10	15–1	11–9	20–8	19–10	18–9	14–5	25–1	23–0	21–9	16–8
	16	11–2	10–11	10–5	8–1	14–8	14–1	13–4	10–3	18–9	17–2	16–3	12–6	22–10	19–11	18–10	14–6
	24	9–9	9–1	8–7	6–7	12–10	11–6	10–10	8–4	16–5	14–0	13–3	10–2	19–9	16–3	15–5	11–10
Southern	12	12–9	12–6	12–3	10–0	16–10	16–6	16–2	12–9	21–6	21–1	19–11	15–1	26–1	25–7	23–4	17–11
Pine	16	11–7	11–5	11–2	8–8	15–3	15–0	14–5	11–0	19–6	19–2	17–3	13–0	23–9	22–10	20–2	15–6
	24	10–2	9–11	9–2	7–1	13–4	13–1	11–9	9–0	17–0	15–8	14–1	10–8	20–9	18–8	16–6	12–8

INSTALLING RAFTERS

The procedure for attaching a gable roof to the existing house roof depends on whether the new ridge runs in the same direction as the old one (parallel) or intersects it (perpendicular).

NEW RIDGE PERPENDICULAR TO OLD

Installing a set of rafters with the new ridge board perpendicular to the old one is more complicated than installing a parallel ridge. Ask some people to help you: It will take at least three sets of hands.

INSTALLING RAFTERS WITH NEW RIDGE BOARD PERPENDICULAR TO OLD

Mark existing roof pitch on ridge board by laying a piece of scrap against it

Strike a chalk line from end of ridge to eave above wall to know where to remove shingles

Pattern rafters

Temporary brace

Leveled ridge board

Strip away roofing and nail 2×4 plates to sheathing

2×4 block

Ridge board notched and installed

Wall plates

Rafters installed

1. Start by cutting two pairs of rafters (see Laying Out the Rafters, page 52). Place one pair at the gable end of the addition, the outside faces of the rafters flush with the end wall. Put a scrap of ridge board material between the top ends of the rafters. Nail the rafters to the cap plates only. Follow the same steps with the other pair of rafters at the opposite end of the addition wall, except nail their bases to the ends of the ceiling joists, as well as the cap plate.

2. Remove the temporary ridge scraps and slide the ridge board up between the pairs of rafters so one end rests on the existing roof and its top is flush with the tops of the rafters. Mark the roof where the bottom of the ridge board touches it.

3. Scribe a line at the end of the ridge board parallel to the slope of the roof. Remove the ridge board and cut it along the scribed line, saving the scrap piece for use later.

4. Snap a chalk line between the ridge-board mark and the two points where the new addition walls intersect the house. Snap a second pair of lines parallel to and 1 foot above the first ones. Remove all of the shingles in the triangular area between the upper set of lines and the eaves.

5. Cut and place two 2×4 plates on the roof sheathing, aligning their top edges on the lines that run between the ridge-board mark and the corners where the addition walls meet the house. To check alignment before nailing, stretch a chalk line across the two sets of common rafters at several points and extend it to the plates. The chalk line should barely touch the top edges of the plates. Adjust the plates and nail them to the roof sheathing.

6. Slide the ridge board back into place and nail it securely to the two plates at the peak. Nail it to the two pairs of common rafters. Slide a 2×4 block under the unsupported end of the ridge board, then nail it in place.

7. Mark the rafter layout (16 inches or 24 inches on center) on both sides of the ridge board and on each wall cap plate, starting at the outer end.

8. Install the rest of the common (full-length) rafters.

9. To mark the spacing for the valley jack rafters along the 2×4 plates on the roof, hook a tape measure on the last common

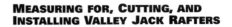

rafter and extend it to the plate, parallel with the ridge board. Mark the point where the rafter-spacing measurement (16 or 24 inches) intersects the top edge of the plate. Slide the tape up the rafter and mark the next rafter location. Mark all rafter locations this way, always keeping the tape measure parallel with the ridge board.

10. Plumb-cut the upper ends of the valley jack rafters at the same angle as the common rafters (see page 52). From the long point of the plumb cut, measure and mark on the rafter the distance between the ridge board and the top edge of the plate at the first layout mark. Scribe the angle to match the seat-cut angle of the bird's mouth cut (90 degrees to the plumb cut, as shown in the illustration at right).

Tilt the blade on your circular saw to match the angle of the ridge-board tail you saved. Cut along the line so that the bottom of the blade angles away from the line, as shown at right.

To minimize waste, cut only one valley rafter from each board, then use the remainder for an opposing rafter. (For example, use the remainder from the longest rafter for the shortest rafter on the opposite side of the roof.) Nail the valley jack rafters in the same way as the common rafters.

11. If you want a gable-end overhang, extend the ridge board, then let in 2×4 lookouts to support an outboard rafter, as shown in the illustration below.

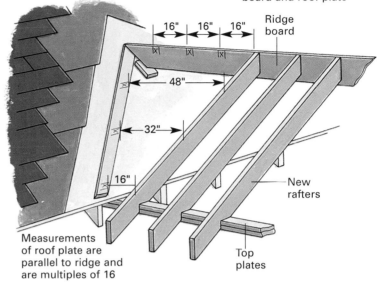

Mark positions of valley jack rafters on ridge board and roof plate

Ridge board

New rafters

Top plates

Measurements of roof plate are parallel to ridge and are multiples of 16

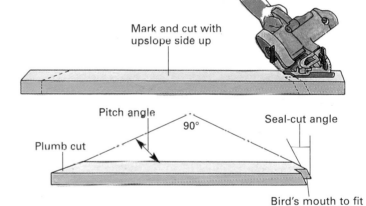

Mark and cut with upslope side up

Pitch angle

90°

Seat-cut angle

Plumb cut

Bird's mouth to fit over roof plate

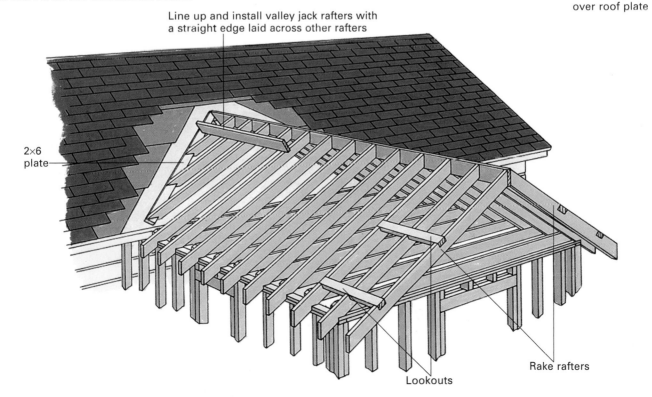

Line up and install valley jack rafters with a straight edge laid across other rafters

2×6 plate

Lookouts

Rake rafters

INSTALLING RAFTERS
continued

INSTALLING RAFTERS WITH NEW RIDGE BOARD PARALLEL TO OLD

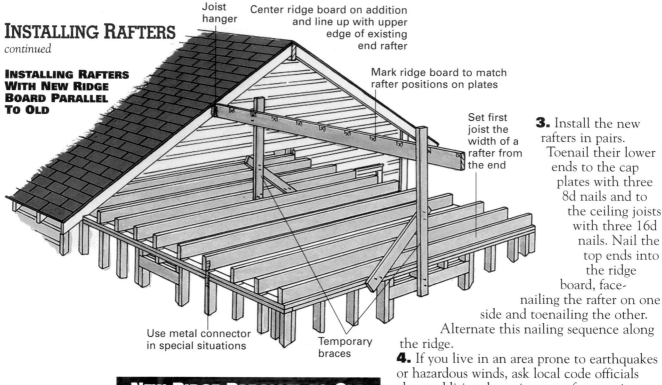

Joist hanger

Center ridge board on addition and line up with upper edge of existing end rafter

Mark ridge board to match rafter positions on plates

Set first joist the width of a rafter from the end

Use metal connector in special situations

Temporary braces

3. Install the new rafters in pairs. Toenail their lower ends to the cap plates with three 8d nails and to the ceiling joists with three 16d nails. Nail the top ends into the ridge board, face-nailing the rafter on one side and toenailing the other. Alternate this nailing sequence along the ridge.

4. If you live in an area prone to earthquakes or hazardous winds, ask local code officials about additional requirements for securing rafters. You may only need to add wood collar ties at the tops of the rafters, or building codes might require metal framing clips and hurricane ties to secure the rafters to the walls and the ridge board.

5. Install the rake (or barge) rafters. If the rafter tails will be covered by fascia boards, extend the fascia boards and the ridge board beyond the end rafters far enough to support the rake rafters. Nail blocks between the rake and end rafters every 16 inches. If there will be no fascia boards, support the rake rafters with 2×4 lookouts let into the last pair of rafters on 2-foot intervals.

6. Nail blocking between the rafters above the cap plates. Where the ceiling or roof will be insulated, leave 1 inch at the tops of the blocking to allow for ventilation.

NEW RIDGE PARALLEL TO OLD

Installing rafters with the ridge parallel to the old one is not as difficult as installing a perpendicular one. Here's how to do it:

1. If the existing roof has an overhang, cut it back to the last rafter that is flush with the framing of the existing end wall.

2. Butt the ridge board to the edge of the last house rafter, holding it in place with a joist hanger. Brace the other end temporarily.

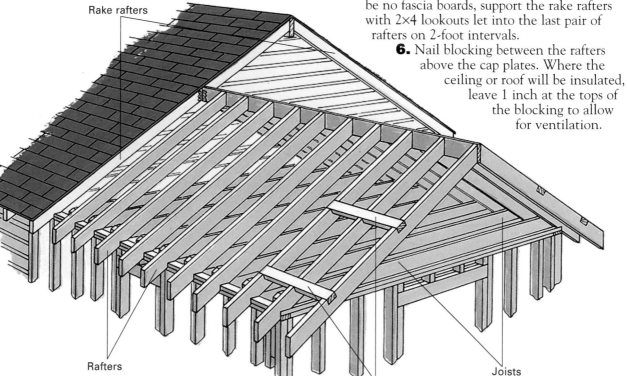

Rake rafters

Rafters

Lookouts

Joists

TRUSSES

Contractors and developers usually build roofs with trusses, prefabricated assemblies of ceiling joists and rafters. Trusses span long distances using small dimensional lumber to save material. Contractors also rely on trusses because they speed roof construction and cut labor costs in half compared to traditional framing methods.

Trusses also eliminate the need for exact measuring and cutting of rafters. A drawback is the loss of usable space under the roof. Common rafters, without the diagonal bracing of trusses, provide open space between the rafters and ceiling joists that can be used for storage or, with enough pitch, living space.

INSTALLATION

You can order trusses through most lumberyards. Take your plans and exact building dimensions with you when you order trusses so the dealer can make sure you get the right ones. Have the trusses delivered the day you plan to install them. Arrange to have the delivery crew place the trusses on top of the walls.

Have at least three persons on hand to install trusses; two to slide the truss ends into place on the cap plates and a third to raise the peak, using a long pole from the ground.

Follow the manufacturer's installation instructions exactly, especially regarding temporary bracing. If the bracing fails, the trusses can fall like dominos, not only damaging them but possibly injuring you or your helpers.

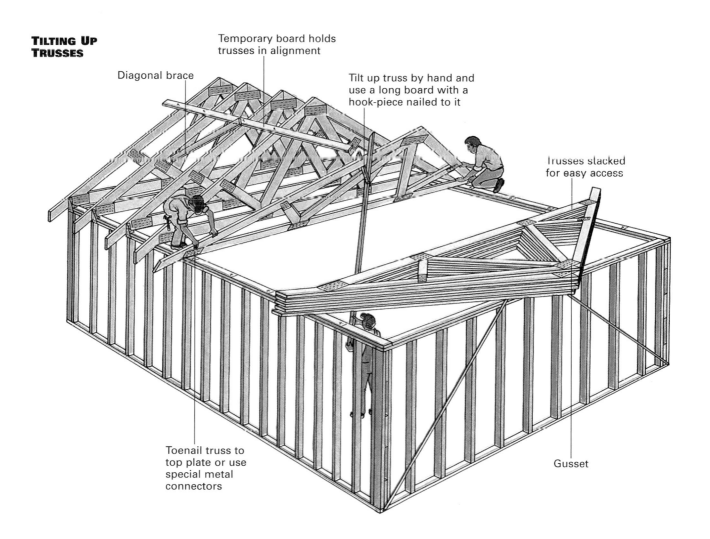

TILTING UP TRUSSES

Diagonal brace

Temporary board holds trusses in alignment

Tilt up truss by hand and use a long board with a hook-piece nailed to it

Trusses stacked for easy access

Toenail truss to top plate or use special metal connectors

Gusset

SHEATHING

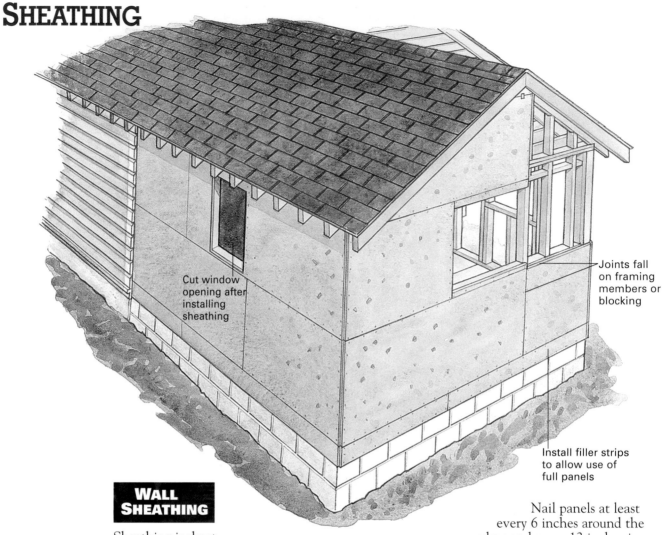

Cut window opening after installing sheathing

Joints fall on framing members or blocking

Install filler strips to allow use of full panels

WALL SHEATHING

Sheathing is sheet material, such as plywood or OSB, which braces the wall and provides a nailing surface for most types of siding.

Diagonal metal straps or let-in 1×4 boards are sometimes used to brace the walls when siding can be applied directly to the studs. But in high-quality construction, walls are usually sheathed with solid material. Some materials, such as textured plywood siding, function as both sheathing and siding, saving money and labor.

Plywood sheathing must be at least ⅜ inch thick; at least ½ inch thick if you will nail shingles or stucco lath to the sheathing. Panels may be installed either horizontally or vertically, but all seams must fall over framing members or blocking. If the height of the framing from mudsill to cap plate is more than 96 inches, install a filler strip of sheathing from just below the mudsill to the midline of the soleplate. Above the filler strip, install full sheets. Always use large sheets as much as possible. Don't patch several scraps together.

Nail panels at least every 6 inches around the edges and every 12 inches in the center with 6d common or box nails. Install blocking behind any seams that do not fall on framing. Check your plans for additional nailing or blocking that might be required in areas where earthquakes or high winds are likely or for construction on a steep hillside.

Cut the sheathing flush with the inside edges of rough openings for windows and doors. You can take careful measurements, lay out the openings on the panel, and cut them before installing the panels. Most builders, however, install full panels, then cut out the openings later with a reciprocating saw.

If you are installing textured plywood siding without additional sheathing and the addition has no soffits, notch the tops of the panels to fit around the rafters. Butt the edge of the siding against the underside of the roof sheathing.

When siding will be installed over studs without sheathing, install permanent diagonal corner bracing on the outside of the studs. Metal straps are stronger and easier to install than 1×4 let-in bracing. The bracing must

SOLID DECK OF PLYWOOD

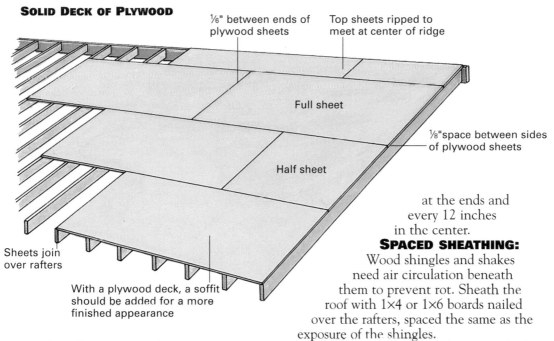

⅛" between ends of plywood sheets

Top sheets ripped to meet at center of ridge

Full sheet

⅛"space between sides of plywood sheets

Half sheet

Sheets join over rafters

With a plywood deck, a soffit should be added for a more finished appearance

cross each wall at 30 to 45 degrees, must connect the top plate and soleplate (or mudsill, if possible), and must be nailed at each stud with a 16d common nail.

ROOF SHEATHING

Install roof sheathing and roofing before the siding in order to weatherproof the addition as soon as possible. Be sure the walls are well braced and the rafters are tied to the walls before sheathing the roof because a strong wind can exert tremendous lift on the sheathed roof.

Sheathing for most roofing materials is ½- or ⅝-inch plywood or OSB. Some roofing materials, such as wood shingles, require spaced sheathing of 1×4 boards.

When planning the roof sheathing, determine if the underside of the sheathing will be visible at the eaves and rake edges or if soffits will conceal it. If it will be visible, use an attractive material for the visible panels, such as plywood siding or V-rustic wood siding, and sheath the rest of the roof with less expensive panels.

PANEL SHEATHING: Install plywood and OSB panels perpendicular to the rafters, staggering the end joints by 4 feet. Leave ⅛-inch gaps at all panel edges to allow for expansion. Slip metal H-shaped panel clips over the panel edges to lock them together between rafters. These clips automatically space the panels and prevent panel deflection when the roof is walked on. Nail the panels with 8d nails every 6 inches

at the ends and every 12 inches in the center.

SPACED SHEATHING: Wood shingles and shakes need air circulation beneath them to prevent rot. Sheath the roof with 1×4 or 1×6 boards nailed over the rafters, spaced the same as the exposure of the shingles.

For instance, if wood shingles are applied with a 5-inch exposure (the amount of the shingle exposed to the weather), the sheathing boards must be spaced 5 inches on-center so the shingle nails can be driven into them. The first 18 inches just above the eaves and 18 inches just below the ridge on each side are usually covered with solid boards for a better nailing surface.

TONGUE-AND-GROOVE SHEATHING: If the sheathing will be exposed inside the house, as with cathedral ceilings, use tongue-and-groove pine or cedar roofers. Install the first board along the eaves with its tongue edge toward the ridge. Use scraps of tongue-and-groove boards as hammering blocks when you knock successive boards into place. Stagger the butt joints, and gap the joints ¹⁄₁₆ inch for expansion when wet.

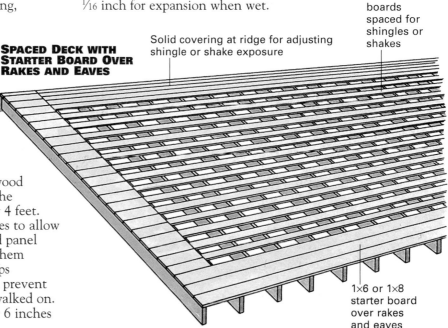

SPACED DECK WITH STARTER BOARD OVER RAKES AND EAVES

Solid covering at ridge for adjusting shingle or shake exposure

1×4 or 1×6 boards spaced for shingles or shakes

1×6 or 1×8 starter board over rakes and eaves

ROOFING

**LAYING
THE ROOF**

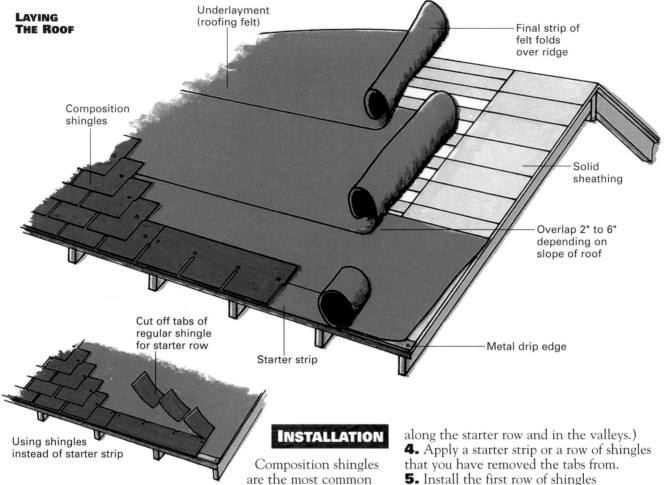

Underlayment
(roofing felt)

Final strip of
felt folds
over ridge

Composition
shingles

Solid
sheathing

Overlap 2" to 6"
depending on
slope of roof

Cut off tabs of
regular shingle
for starter row

Starter strip

Metal drip edge

Using shingles
instead of starter strip

INSTALLATION

Composition shingles are the most common and are probably easiest to install of the many roofing materials. They come in a variety of colors, weights, tab sizes, textures, and edge configurations. The most durable have a fiberglass core, which also gives them a better fire rating than shingles with a felt core.

The shingles for an addition are applied the same as for any new construction. The only difference is in joining the new shingles to the old. Here is how to install them:

1. Nail aluminum or galvanized-steel drip edge along the eaves. The drip edge prevents rain runoff from running back under the shingles and protects the edge of the sheathing from weathering.

2. Starting at the bottom, cover the roof with 15-pound felt underlayment lapped 4 inches (19 inches for roof slopes of less than 3 in 12). Keep the printed lines on the felt parallel to the eaves; they will be reference lines for shingling. Staple the felt to the sheathing, but not excessively.

3. Nail additional drip edge over the felt at the rake edges to protect the sheathing edges. (Some areas require ice and water shield along the starter row and in the valleys.)

4. Apply a starter strip or a row of shingles that you have removed the tabs from.

5. Install the first row of shingles with the full shingles offset horizontally by half a tab (6 inches).

6. As you work up the roof slope, maintain a consistent pattern in lining up grooves between individual tabs. The easiest installation is to split the gaps—offset each course by 6 inches. This pattern shows deviations and mistakes more clearly, however. A 4-inch pattern gives a strong diagonal look, wears better than a 6-inch pattern, and is recommended for slopes of less than 4 in 12. Professionals sometimes use a 5-inch pattern, which looks more random.

7. If the new roof extends from the gable end of the old roof, start each course at the intersection and maintain the same pattern as the old roof. For a more durable seam, weave new shingles into old by removing partial shingles from the end of each old course and continuing with a new full shingle.

8. If the new roof is perpendicular to the old one, the intersection will form two valleys. There are two methods of roofing a valley: open (shingles don't run across it) and closed (shingles are laced across it). For an open valley, install metal valley flashing or

90-pound roll roofing in the valley. Start roll roofing with a half-width (18 inches) face down, followed by a full width (36 inches) face up. As you lay each course of shingles, flare the valley slightly outward for better water flow.

9. To form a closed valley, flash the valley with metal or a full sheet (36 inches) of roll roofing laid upside down to minimize cracking. Interweave the shingles of alternating courses over the valley and at least 1 foot up the opposite side. Trim the bottom of the final shingle of each course about 2 inches to keep water from collecting against it.

10. At the top, cut the tabs from shingles and lay the tabs along the ridge, overlapping them by 6 inches. If winds usually blow from one direction, lap the shingles in the direction that will minimize water penetration. Split the last shingle where it butts up against the house roof, and tuck the two flaps up under the row of house shingles.

For more information about roofing, see *Ortho's All About Roofing and Siding Basics.*

STEP FLASHING

Where a roof butts against a house wall, install flashing this way to prevent rain from running down the wall and under the roofing:

1. Strip the siding from the wall above the junction with the roof.

2. Run roofing felt 4 inches up the wall, or install an L-shape strip of 10-inch flashing over the felt.

3. On top of each course of composition shingles, nail a step flashing with its base 5 inches above the bottom of the tab. Nail

INSTALLING A FULL-LACE CLOSED VALLEY

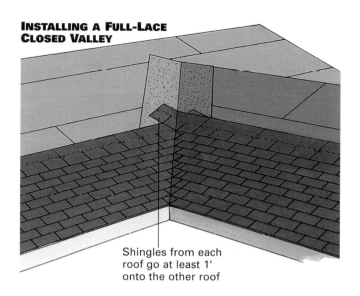

Shingles from each roof go at least 1' onto the other roof

the flashing only at its top so the nails will be covered by the next shingle course.

4. After the whole roof has been shingled and flashed, reinstall the siding, trimmed so its bottom edge clears the roofing by 1 inch.

VENT FLASHING

Flashing prevents rainwater from entering the attic where vent pipes go through the roof. Neoprene flashing boots are easy to install. Purchase a boot for the pipe size, then install the flashing like a shingle. Install the roofing as far as you can, then slip the boot over the pipe and nail its upper corners. Lay the next course of shingles over the top edge of the flashing, as shown in the bottom illustration.

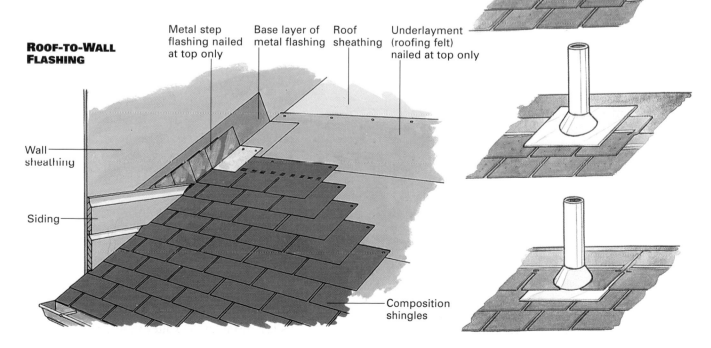

ROOF-TO-WALL FLASHING

Metal step flashing nailed at top only

Base layer of metal flashing

Roof sheathing

Underlayment (roofing felt) nailed at top only

Wall sheathing

Siding

Composition shingles

THE FINAL DETAILS

INSTALLING WINDOWS

SELECTING WINDOWS

Windows in the addition should complement the existing house windows. But there's more to selecting windows than appearance. Energy efficiency and maintenance requirements are important factors to consider. Keep in mind all the functions of a window.

FUNCTIONS: Windows keep out weather, noise, insects, burglars, and other unwanted intrusions. At the same time, windows admit summer breezes, winter sunshine, year-round daylight, and, often, a view of the outside.

THERMAL PERFORMANCE: The most energy-efficient windows are glazed with low-E glass, which has a microscopically thin coating of metal oxides that moderates heat transmission. The coating allows most solar radiation—visible light and heat—to pass through the glass while blocking long-wave radiation—the heat that radiates from surfaces. A double-glazed window of low-E glass can lower energy costs year-round.

Look for a National Fenestration Rating Council (NFRC) label, which lists a window's U-factor and other efficiency ratings. The American Architectural Manufacturers Association (AAMA) and Window and Door Manufacturer's Association (WDMA) rate windows for air infiltration, water resistance, and other qualities. Window dealers can provide rating information for their lines.

MATERIALS: High-quality windows are available in four materials:
- solid wood
- solid vinyl
- vinyl-clad wood
- aluminum-clad wood

Solid-wood windows, traditional favorites, require the most maintenance. Solid-vinyl windows are maintenance-free, but don't have the look or feel of wood. Vinyl- and aluminum-clad windows need no exterior maintenance and have the warm feel of wood on the interior.

CODE REQUIREMENTS

SAFETY GLAZING
Safety glazing, such as plastic or tempered glass, is required in certain locations, such as:
- entry doors, except jalousies
- patio doors
- swinging doors
- storm doors
- unframed swinging doors
- doors and enclosures for tubs, showers, hot tubs, saunas, steam rooms, and whirlpools, where the bottom of the glazing is less than 60 inches above the drain
- where a single pane larger than 9 square feet is within 36 inches horizontally of a walking surface, its bottom is less than 18 inches above the floor, and its top is more than 36 inches above the floor
- all glazings in railings

EXCEPTIONS
Safety glass is not required in these situations:
- door openings less than 3 inches in diameter
- leaded glass panels
- faceted and decorative glass
- glazing in a panel where there is a permanent barrier between a door and the panel
- glazing in a panel where there is a protective bar 34 to 38 inches above the floor that can withstand a horizontal pressure of 50 pounds per linear foot
- exterior panes of multipane window units when the bottom of the pane is at least 25 feet above grade, roof, or walking surface
- louvered windows and jalousies with glass louvers at least $3/16$ inch thick and no more than 48 inches long with smooth edges
- mirrors mounted on flush or panel doors
- mirrors mounted or hung on walls

WINDOW DIMENSIONS

When framing rough openings for windows and doors, it's best to have the windows and doors on hand. If the windows are not on site, double-check the manufacturer's specified rough-opening sizes with your supplier. The rough opening is usually ½ inch wider and taller than the window dimensions.

Before installation, measure both diagonals of the rough opening to make sure it is square. If the opening is out of square by more than ¼ inch, adjust the framing. The rough sill must be level; shims can compensate for a slight slope.

Most windows include exterior casing, simplifying the exterior trim and siding installation. The siding simply butts against the edge of the casing. Many vinyl- and aluminum-clad windows offer the choice of casing or no casing. With no casing, the siding butts against the thin nailing flange.

INSTALLATION

Staple 6-inch-wide flashing paper across the bottom of the rough opening and along both sides, so the side pieces overlap the bottom piece and all inside edges are flush with the opening. Place flashing paper across the top after the window is in position.

Caulk the backs of the window casings or the nailing flanges of metal or vinyl windows. Then, with at least two people, one inside and one outside, set the window into the opening. The inside person levels the window frame with shims, while the outside person steadies the window and nails it in place.

From the inside, place shims between the side jambs and the studs. If specified in the manufacturer's instructions, drive casing nails through the jambs and shims into the studs, toenailing from the edges of the jambs rather than face-nailing. Stuff fiberglass insulation loosely between the jambs and studs.

Drill holes through the casing or the nailing flange, if not predrilled. Nail wood casings with 12d hot-dip galvanized casing nails. Nail metal or vinyl nailing flanges with galvanized roofing nails.

If the window has wood casings, install a metal Z-flashing above the head casing, then install the final piece of flashing paper to overlap the Z-flashing and the side paper flashings or flange. The window is now ready for the installation of wall siding.

WINDOW STYLES

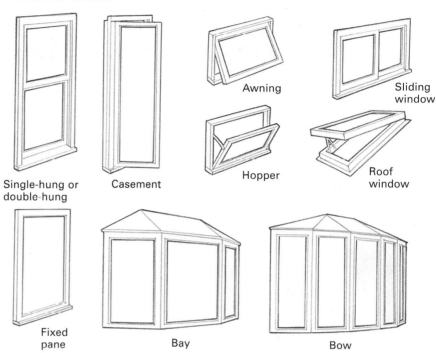

Single-hung or double-hung

Casement

Awning

Hopper

Sliding window

Roof window

Fixed pane

Bay

Bow

WINDOW DIMENSIONS

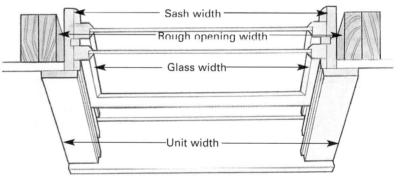

Sash width

Rough opening width

Glass width

Unit width

INSTALLING WINDOW WITH NAILING FLANGE

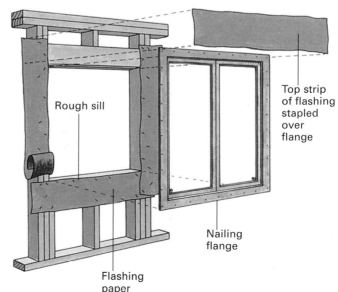

Rough sill

Top strip of flashing stapled over flange

Nailing flange

Flashing paper

INSTALLING SKYLIGHTS

A skylight, or a roof window, is one of the most effective and dramatic design features you can incorporate into your addition. Daylight from overhead is usually stronger than horizontal light, and the skylight introduces it into the interior of a room, so a skylight is about four times more effective than a window for lighting a room. Follow the detailed installation instructions provided by the skylight manufacturer. Here are typical installation steps.

FRAMING

Most skylights require more than one rafter space for the opening. Cut the rafters involved back 6 inches farther than the rough-opening height of the skylight to allow for double headers at top and bottom. Double the full-length rafters on each side, and support the ends of the cut rafters with the double headers, as shown below.

CURB

Some skylights mount on a curb that raises the glazing above the surface of the roof. If the skylight doesn't have an integral curb, build a simple rectangle of 2×6s. The outside dimensions of the frame should be 3/8 inch shorter than the inside dimensions of the skylight frame. Remove the shingles around the opening. Lay the curb over the opening and check that it's square by measuring both diagonals. Toenail it into the roof sheathing with 8d nails.

FLASHING

Apply roofing up to the bottom of the curb and lay the bottom flashing collar over the roofing. Nail it to the sides of the curb. As you continue shingling up the roof beside the curb, finish each row of shingles with a piece of step flashing. Cover the flashing with the next row of shingles. (See Step Flashing on page 63.) Finish the top of the curb with another metal collar and carry the next row of shingles over its top flange.

SKYLIGHT

To install the skylight, lay a bead of silicone caulk along the top edge of the curb and place the skylight down over it. Drive aluminum nails with neoprene washers through the sides of the skylight into the curb.

FRAMING OPTIONS

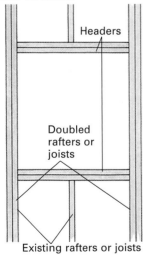
Headers

Doubled rafters or joists

Existing rafters or joists

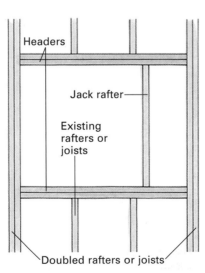
Headers

Jack rafter

Existing rafters or joists

Doubled rafters or joists

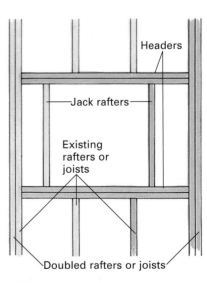
Headers

Jack rafters

Existing rafters or joists

Doubled rafters or joists

INSTALLING A CURB

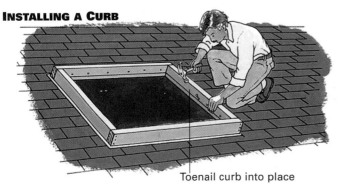
Toenail curb into place

INSTALLING A SKYLIGHT

Caulk

INSTALLING DOORS

PREHUNG DOORS

Unless you are an experienced carpenter, purchase prehung doors. These units come with the door, jambs, hinges, stop, and casings all preassembled. The door is also usually predrilled for a lockset.

Several versions are available at lumberyards and home centers. For a conventional, $4\frac{1}{2}$-inch-thick interior wall ($3\frac{1}{2}$-inch studs plus two layers of $\frac{1}{2}$-inch drywall), get the standard unit with $4\frac{9}{16}$-inch-wide jambs. For a wall of different thickness, get a split-jamb prehung door. These have two-part telescoping jambs that can accommodate wall thicknesses of:
- $4\frac{1}{8}$ to $4\frac{11}{16}$ inches (drywall)
- $4\frac{1}{4}$ to $5\frac{1}{4}$ inches (plaster wall)
- $6\frac{3}{16}$ to $6\frac{15}{16}$ inches (wide wall)

INSTALLING THE DOOR

1. Remove the packing and the casing if it is already installed on the unit.
2. Knock out the hinge pins to separate the door from the jamb. Trim off the excess at the tops of the side jambs so they fit into the rough opening with clearance of at least $\frac{1}{2}$ inch.
3. Center the jamb in the rough opening. Place pairs of shim shingles between the hinge-side jamb and the studs at each hinge location. Drive a 12d finish nail through the jamb and shims at the top hinge. Drive it all the way except for the last $\frac{1}{4}$ inch.
4. Check the hinge jamb for plumb with a 4-foot level, adjusting the shims in or out until the entire jamb is straight and plumb. Drive 12d finish nails through the center of the jamb at each hinge location. Then shim and nail it at the top and bottom.
5. Level the head jamb by holding a carpenter's square against the hinge jamb and head jamb. Adjust the shims, then nail the head jamb to the header through the shims.
6. Measure the width between the side jambs at the top of the door, making sure the door closes easily. Shim the latch-side jamb at the top, bottom, middle, and two intermediate points to maintain this width. Nail it through the shims.
7. Hang the door and close it from time to time as you finish nailing the latch jamb. Score the protruding ends of the shims with a utility knife and snap them off.

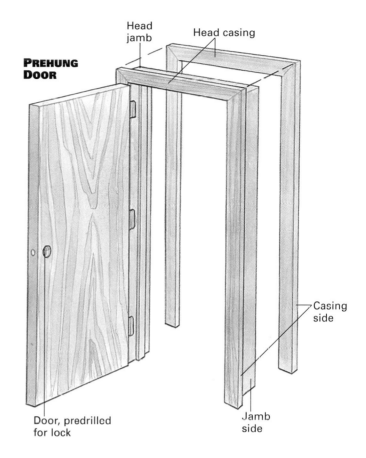

PREHUNG DOOR

Head jamb

Head casing

Casing side

Jamb side

Door, predrilled for lock

8. Replace the casing you removed in the first step. Nail it to the jamb and into the wall studs with 6d finish nails. Nail the casing on the other side to the wall studs.

DOOR LOCKSET

Door locksets offer three degrees of security:
- passage set—no lock
- privacy set—lockable from the inside only; good for bedrooms and bathrooms
- security set—lockable from inside and outside; suitable for an entry door or an interior door into the garage, for example

Install the lockset following the manufacturer's instructions.

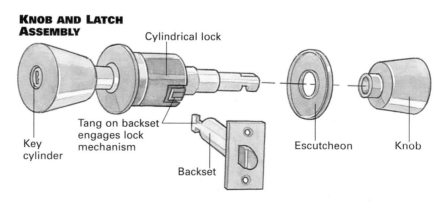

KNOB AND LATCH ASSEMBLY

Cylindrical lock

Key cylinder

Tang on backset engages lock mechanism

Backset

Escutcheon

Knob

SIDING

It is usually best to match the siding on the addition to the siding already on the house. Sidings on older homes may be hard to match, however. Begin your search early so if you need to, you can make changes before it's time to install the siding.

A lumberyard or mill that does custom milling may be able to match an obsolete or unusual pattern. Architectural salvage firms might have what you need, too. If you can't match your house siding, be careful when you choose a different material for the addition. The pattern should be close enough for the addition to look like it's part of the house.

If the sidings aren't identical, you can minimize the differences by painting the new siding to match the house. Then use the trim, roofing, and window styles to maintain continuity. Or you can hide the junction of the two siding styles—where the discrepancy is most obvious—behind shrubbery, a trellis, or a screen fence.

If the house siding is weathered and worn, consider siding both the house and addition with the same material. If the proportions of the new addition allow, you could install a siding different from what's on the house for a contrast. Mixed materials can be attractive, but it's often best to get professional design advice beforehand.

Here are some siding materials to consider:

HARDBOARD: Hardboard lap siding comes in a variety of widths and textures. It is available plain, primed (ready for the paint of your choice), or prepainted. Paint unprimed siding within 30 days; primed within 60 days.

Install the siding with 8d stainless-steel or galvanized siding nails, driven only into studs. Adjacent lengths can butt together; nail the siding at both top and bottom at the joints. Leave a ⅛-inch gap around doors and windows and at corner boards. Caulk the gap before painting with paintable caulk or caulk it after painting.

WOOD SHINGLE: Cedar shingles are a traditional siding material. Many grades are available in red or white cedar. Use only No. 1 red cedar or Extra grade white cedar shingles for siding.

Exposure for the common 16-inch single should not exceed 7½ inches. Fasten the shingles with two 3d shingle nails, 1 inch from the edges and just high enough to be covered by the following course.

Shingles are usually treated with a clear preservative or left unfinished. They can be stained or painted, too.

HORIZONTAL WOOD: Most horizontal wood sidings are redwood or red cedar. White pine is popular in the Northeast.

The most common problem with horizontal sidings is curling and nail-popping, caused by moisture and weather. Edge-grain or radial-sawn siding boards resist curling, but the best prevention is to prime both the front and back of the siding before installation.

Fasten horizontal wood sidings with stainless-steel siding nails long enough to penetrate into the studs 1½ inches.

HARDBOARD SIDING

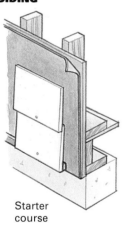

Starter course

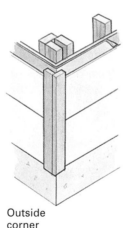

Outside corner

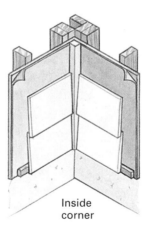

Inside corner

WOOD SHINGLE SIDING

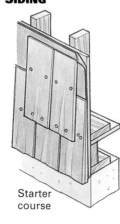

Starter course

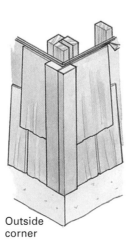

Outside corner

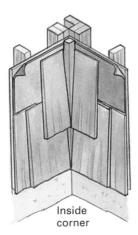

Inside corner

VINYL AND ALUMINUM:

These nonwood sidings are the most practical of all of the siding products. They are inexpensive, dimensionally uniform, modular, predrilled, lightweight, and maintenance-free. Installation is simple, as long as you follow the manufacturer's instructions. They have their drawbacks, however. Some people think nonwood siding is so uniform it doesn't look natural. Also, metal or vinyl siding sometimes cracks or dents when struck.

The color is incorporated in vinyl siding. Aluminum siding comes prepainted from the factory.

VERTICAL WOOD: Vertical sidings

are generally chosen for their rustic look. Rough-sawn lumber not only is more rustic looking, but it's less expensive and holds stain and paint better than surfaced (planed) lumber. For uniform thickness, vertical sidings are often surfaced on one side.

The best source for rough-sawn siding is a small sawmill. Small mills often don't advertise, so ask local contractors for referrals.

Fasten vertical wood sidings with stainless-steel siding nails long enough to penetrate the sheathing and the studs by 1½ inches.

INSTALLING SIDING

Siding is applied like the shingles of a roof—each layer overlaps the one below it so that water flows downward over the surface and never reaches the sheathing beneath. Lapped underlayment (building felt) usually backs up the siding. Many builders now substitute house wrap for underlayment. Polypropylene wraps let the wall breathe while reducing air infiltration. For detailed instructions about installing siding, see *Ortho's All About Roofing and Siding Basics.*

NAILING PATTERNS FOR HORIZONTAL WOOD SIDING (SIDE VIEW)

CORNER CONSTRUCTION

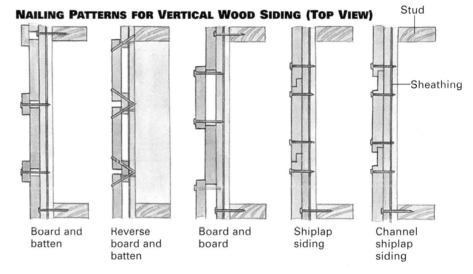

Bevel siding

Rabbeted bevel siding

Tongue-and-groove siding

V-groove siding

Stud

Sheathing

Outside corner

Sheathing Stud

Siding

Inside corner

NAILING PATTERNS FOR VERTICAL WOOD SIDING (TOP VIEW)

Board and batten

Reverse board and batten

Board and board

Shiplap siding

Channel shiplap siding

Stud

Sheathing

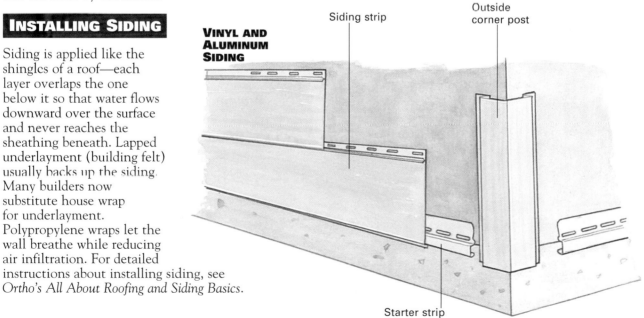

Siding strip

Outside corner post

VINYL AND ALUMINUM SIDING

Starter strip

ACCESS FROM THE HOUSE

If an existing exterior doorway opens from the house into the addition, you can simply swap the exterior door for an interior door in the same jamb and replace the threshold. Since interior doors are thinner than exterior doors (1⅜ inches thick for interior, 1¾ inches for exterior doors), you may want to replace the jambs. If the existing exterior door is in good condition and fits the style of the room, you could just leave it in place.

If your design calls for moving or enlarging the door, you will have to cut a new doorway. For an addition that enlarges an existing room, you will have to remove part of— and perhaps all of—the common wall.

PREPARATION

Whether you are using the existing door, creating a new doorway, or removing the entire wall, strip the exterior siding from the house wall. If you are creating a new doorway or creating a large opening, reroute any affected wiring and plumbing before altering the framing.

CREATING A NEW DOORWAY

When installing a new door, verify its exact size before framing the rough opening. The rough opening for a door is usually 2 inches wider than the door to allow for two side jambs, each

DOOR FRAMING

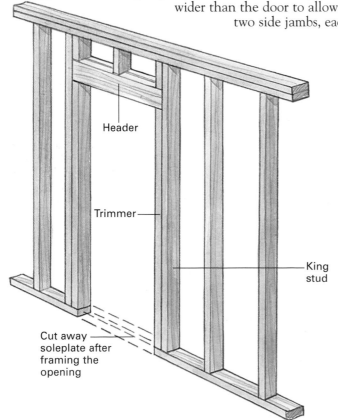

Header

Trimmer

King stud

Cut away soleplate after framing the opening

¾ inch thick, plus ½-inch clearance. The rough-opening height is usually 6 feet 10 inches above the subfloor to make room for a 6-foot-8-inch door, plus 2 inches for the head jamb, finish flooring, and adequate clearance. Allow another ¾ inch for thick tile or carpet.

If you are installing a prehung door, make the rough opening ½ inch wider and ½ inch taller than the assembled unit.

Here's how to frame the opening:

1. Place the hinge side of the door against an existing plumb stud when possible. Otherwise, cut and toenail a new king stud. Set it 1½ inches past the edge of the proposed rough opening to allow for a trimmer stud.

2. Cut and face-nail the trimmer stud (usually 82 inches long) in place with a pair of 12d common nails every 16 inches.

3. Install the second king stud. Mark its location on the top and bottom plates by measuring from the first trimmer stud a distance equal to the rough-opening width plus 1½ inches.

4. Cut the second 2×4 trimmer. Its top should be level with the top of the first trimmer. Do not install the trimmer yet.

5. Mark each king stud 5½ inches above its trimmer. Then snap a chalk line between the marks across the intermediate studs. Cut the intermediate studs at that chalk mark.

6. Measure the distance between the king studs to find the length of the header. Assemble the header from two lengths of 2×6, with ½-inch plywood between them. Snug the assembled header up against the cut intermediate studs by setting one end on the already-installed trimmer and forcing up the other header end with the new trimmer.

7. Using 8d common nails, toenail the header to the king studs and to the tops of the trimmer studs, then install cripple studs above both header ends. Toenail the remaining cripple studs, and remove the section of soleplate between the trimmers with a handsaw or reciprocating saw.

CREATING A LARGE OPENING

Before you remove a wall, make sure you know if it is a nonbearing wall or a bearing wall that supports the roof or upstairs floors. Often, if the joists above the wall run perpendicular to the top plate, it is a bearing wall. Consult a contractor if you aren't sure. You can remove a nonbearing wall with no further preparation. If you are removing a bearing wall, follow this procedure.

1. First size the beam that will replace the wall. If it is to support just the ceiling and the roof, use the table, Exterior Wall Headers Supporting Roof and Ceiling, on page 47.

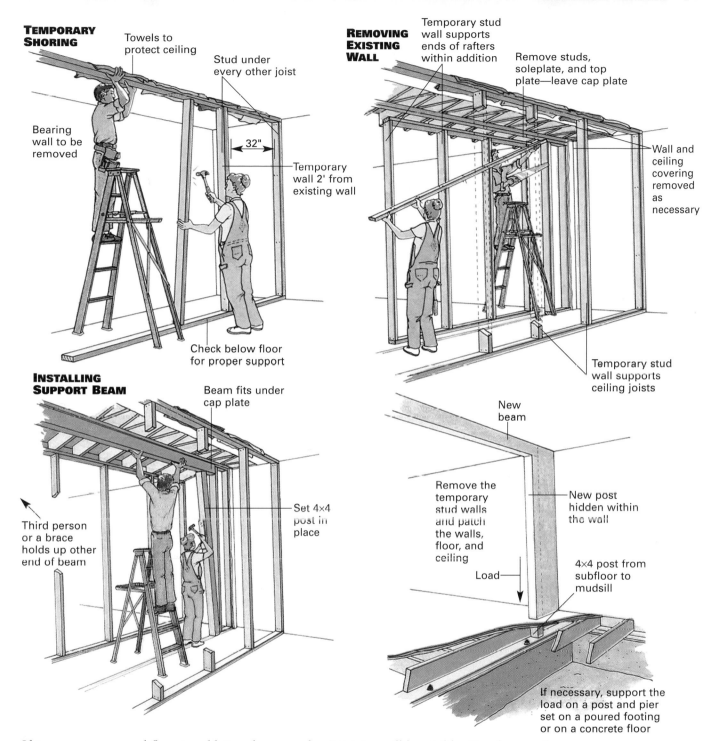

TEMPORARY SHORING

Towels to protect ceiling

Stud under every other joist

Bearing wall to be removed

32"

Temporary wall 2' from existing wall

Check below floor for proper support

REMOVING EXISTING WALL

Temporary stud wall supports ends of rafters within addition

Remove studs, soleplate, and top plate—leave cap plate

Wall and ceiling covering removed as necessary

Temporary stud wall supports ceiling joists

INSTALLING SUPPORT BEAM

Beam fits under cap plate

Third person or a brace holds up other end of beam

Set 4×4 post in place

New beam

Remove the temporary stud walls and patch the walls, floor, and ceiling

Load

New post hidden within the wall

4×4 post from subfloor to mudsill

If necessary, support the load on a post and pier set on a poured footing or on a concrete floor

If it supports a second floor in addition, have an engineer determine the beam size.

2. Set temporary shoring on the house side of the wall to support the wall's load. Set similar shoring under the rafter ends (if any) on the addition side to support the roof load.

3. Remove the covering from the wall. Mark the dimensions of the new rough opening on the top plate and the soleplate.

4. Remove the studs, then cut and remove the soleplate and the top plate at the marks, leaving the cap plate undisturbed.

5. Next, install a 4×4 post to support one end of the beam. Measure and cut it carefully, especially if the joint between the beam and

the 4×4 joint will be visible. Cut the post for the other end, but do not install it yet. Make sure the new posts are supported all the way to the foundation.

6. Get some help to lift the beam into place, resting one end on top of the first 4×4. Snug the other end up by tapping the second 4×4 into position under it with a sledgehammer. Use a scrap piece of wood to protect the 4×4 from the hammer.

7. Nail down through the cap plate into the beam at each ceiling joist. After the beam has been secured, remove the temporary shoring and finish the beam and stud walls.

WIRING

Wiring an addition is less complicated than wiring a house. First, the most difficult installation—the service entrance—is already done. Second, the existing circuits serve as examples of how to run new circuits. As a homeowner, you are allowed to do wiring in your own home (as long as you comply with the code). This section will help you understand how the electrical system of your home works.

WHAT IS A CIRCUIT?

An electrical circuit is a loop of wires, originating at a circuit breaker or fuse in the service entrance box and serving one or more electrical devices.

Electrical current—a stream of electrons—flows through a wire (the hot wire) from a voltage source, passes through one or more electrical devices, such as a lamp, a radio, or a circular saw, and returns to the source through another wire (the neutral wire). Receptacles provide a convenient way to

A SIMPLE CIRCUIT DIAGRAM

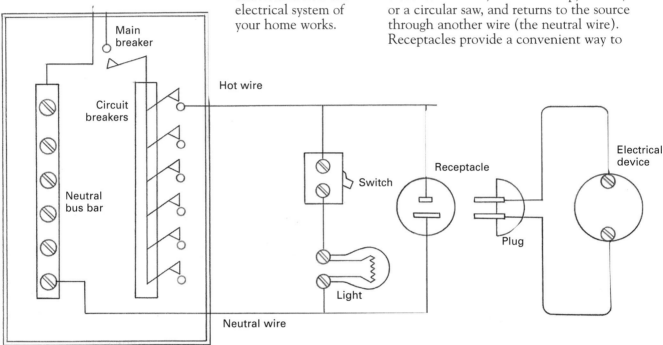

CODE REQUIREMENTS: CIRCUITS

CONVENIENCE OUTLETS
Convenience receptacles are required in every habitable room and must be spaced so that no point along a wall that's more than 2 feet wide is more than 6 feet from an outlet.

GFCI
Ground-Fault Circuit Interrupter protection is required for all receptacles in these locations:
■ bathrooms
■ within 6 feet of a kitchen sink
■ unfinished basements, except outlets dedicated to appliances and sump pumps
■ garages, except outlets dedicated to appliances
■ crawl spaces

■ outdoors when accessible from ground level; such receptacles are required at the front and rear of a dwelling

KITCHEN OUTLETS
The kitchen, pantry, and dining room must have at least two 20-amp small appliance circuits. Refrigerators and freezers can use these circuits. Outlets must be provided for any countertop 12 inches wide or wider, and no point along a countertop can be more than 24 inches from an outlet.

BATHROOM OUTLETS
Bathrooms must have at least one outlet next to each lavatory, but a

single outlet between two lavatories is permitted. All bathroom outlets must be GFCI-protected.

SWITCHED LIGHTING OUTLETS
There must be at least one outlet controlled by a wall switch in every habitable room, bathroom, hallway, stairway, and wired garage.

MISCELLANEOUS OUTLETS
A convenience outlet is required in these locations:
■ laundry room
■ basement
■ attached garage
■ detached garage with power
■ hallways 10 feet long or longer

A TYPICAL WIRING PLAN

Circuits

- Lights: Kitchen, porch, and family room, 15 amp or 20 amp
- Small appliance, 20 amp
- Small appliance, 20 amp
- Range and oven: 20 amp to 50 amp
- Dishwasher, 20 amp
- Garbage disposer, 20 amp

Symbols

- Light
- Switch
- Outlet
- Circuits

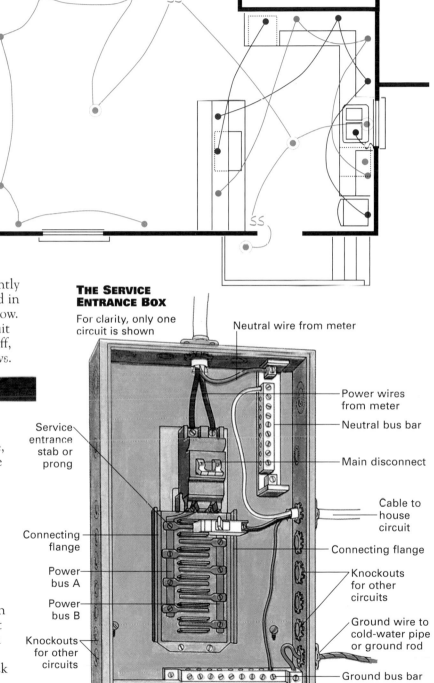

connect appliances to the circuit. Some items, such as light fixtures, are permanently wired into the circuit. A switch installed in the hot wire can interrupt the current flow. Turning a switch on completes the circuit and current flows. When the switch is off, the circuit is broken and no current flows.

THE WIRING PLAN

Develop a wiring plan before you start. Without thinking of how the wires will run, plot the location of each receptacle, light fixture, switch, and fixed appliance on your floor plan. Then link them together into circuits, as shown at the top of the page.

Except for fixed appliances, which have their own dedicated circuits, you should be able to wire an entire small addition on one general-purpose circuit, which usually has 10 to 13 fixtures on it. If the house is wired so that lights and outlets are all on separate circuits, extend one of the light circuits for the addition lights and add a new circuit for the outlets.

Plan where you will run the wires back to the main breaker panel or a subpanel. This is usually done under the floor or in the attic.

THE SERVICE ENTRANCE

The service entrance is the gray steel box that contains circuit breakers for the house. The service entrance cable from the power line—a bare (neutral) wire and two black (hot) wires—usually enters at the top. Both hot

THE SERVICE ENTRANCE BOX

For clarity, only one circuit is shown

- Neutral wire from meter
- Power wires from meter
- Neutral bus bar
- Main disconnect
- Cable to house circuit
- Connecting flange
- Knockouts for other circuits
- Ground wire to cold-water pipe or ground rod
- Ground bus bar
- Service entrance stab or prong
- Connecting flange
- Power bus A
- Power bus B
- Knockouts for other circuits

wires go to the main disconnect switch. The output of the main disconnect is connected to two power buses, running down the middle of the box. The bare wire of the entrance cable connects to the neutral bus bar in the box. At the other side, or at the bottom of the box, is the ground bus bar, which may or may not be directly connected to the neutral bus bar.

WIRING
continued

To add a circuit to the entrance box, first turn off the main disconnect. Connect a circuit breaker of the type specified for the box to one of the buses. Remove one of the circular knockouts, install a connector clamp, and thread the cable through it. Strip the cable sheathing back and connect the black wire to the breaker, the white wire to the neutral bus bar, and the bare wire to the ground bus bar. Turn on the main disconnect and the new breaker to energize the circuit.

BOXES

Electrical connections and devices such as switches and outlets must be contained in a box. The first step in wiring a circuit is to install the boxes; you can use metal or plastic ones. Plastic boxes are less expensive and do not require grounding. Metal boxes provide a wider margin for error in cutting out drywall but are more expensive and must be grounded.

BOX SHAPE: The shape of the box depends on its use. Boxes for switches and receptacles are rectangular. Metal switch boxes can be ganged—joined together. Plastic boxes are available in multiple-device sizes. Junction boxes are usually square. Round and octagonal boxes are used for lamp fixtures, sometimes for junction boxes. Utility or handy boxes are intended for surface mounting. Some devices, such as wall heaters and recessed lights, have their own electrical boxes built into the housing.

BOX SIZE: The National Electric Code specifies how many wires and fittings can safely fit into a box. The table at right shows how big a box you will need. When using the table, calculate the number of conductors by using the following rules:

- Each hot or neutral wire (black, white, or red) counts as a conductor.
- All grounding wires together count as one conductor.
- Each device or fixture counts as one conductor.
- All internal wire clamps and fixture studs together count as one conductor.

CAPACITY OF BOXES

Number of Conductors That a Box Can Contain

Box Shape	Dim. in inches	AWG Wire Size 8	10	12	14
Square	4×1¼	6	7	8	9
	4×1½	7	8	9	10
	4×2⅛	10	12	13	15
	4 11/16×1¼	8	10	11	12
	4 11/16×1½	9	11	13	14
Round	4×1¼	4	5	5	6
&	4×1½	5	6	6	7
Octagon	4×2⅛	7	8	9	10
Rectangle	3×2×1½	2	3	3	3
	3×2×2	3	4	4	5
	3×2×2¼	3	4	4	5
	3×2×2½	4	5	5	6
	3×2×2¾	4	5	6	7
	3×2×3½	6	7	8	9

TYPICAL BOXES AND ACCESSORIES

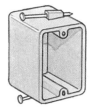

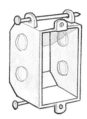

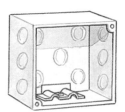

HEIGHT ABOVE THE FLOOR: The code does not specify the height of the center of a box above the floor. The following dimensions are commonly used:
SWITCH: 44 to 48 inches
RECEPTACLE: 12 inches
BASEBOARD HEATER: 6 inches
CEILING LIGHT: center of ceiling
JUNCTION BOX: wherever accessible; box cannot be concealed inside walls

WIRE AND CABLE

Circuits are run with cable, which consists of two or more conductors in a sheath. The cable is labeled with the type of sheathing, the size and number of conductors, and whether it contains a bare ground wire.

In NM 12/2 w/G, for instance, NM means nonmetallic (plastic) sheathing, 12/2 means two 12-gauge conductors, and w/G indicates a separate ground conductor in the cable.
AMPACITY (AMP CAPACITY): All wire, even copper wire, resists the flow of electricity. This resistance results in heat and a drop in voltage. The heat is proportional to the current (in amps) squared; voltage drop is proportional to the current and the length of the cable. Heat from excessive current flow could melt the plastic insulation around the wires, allowing the wires to touch—a short circuit. To prevent this, the load on the circuit and the circuit breaker (or fuse) protecting the circuit are limited by the ampacity of the wire (see table below).
WIRE COLOR CODE: So that you can readily identify wires in a cable to make connections, the insulation is color-coded:

BLACK: hot wire; connects to the brass (or darkest) screw terminal on a device
RED: the second hot wire (the other one is the black one) in a three-wire, 220-volt circuit; also used sometimes in three-way switch circuits
WHITE: neutral wire; connects to the silver screw terminal
BARE: grounding wire; connects to the green screw terminal
GREEN: fixture grounding wire; connects to green screw

RECEPTACLES

Plug and receptacle prongs are arranged differently for each combination of current and voltage to prevent plugging an appliance into a circuit with the wrong current or voltage supply. Always install the receptacle that corresponds to the capacity of the circuit which serves it.

SWITCHES

You will find four types of wall switches in the wiring section of your hardware store or home center.
■ Single-Pole: two terminals on the same side; controls a single circuit from a single location; toggle labeled ON/OFF.
■ Double-Pole: two terminals on each side; can control a 220-volt circuit or two 110-volt circuits; toggle labeled ON/OFF.
■ Three-Way: three terminals; controls a single circuit from two locations; toggle not labeled.
■ Four-Way: four terminals; controls a single circuit from three locations; toggle not labeled.

RECEPTACLES

120 volt
15 amp

120 volt
20 amp

120/240 volt
30 amp

240 volt
20 amp

240 volt
30 amp

120/240 volt
50 amp

AMPACITY OF CABLES

Wire Size	Max. Amps/ Voltage Drop per 100 feet Types T&TW	Type SE
14	15A / 3.7V	–
12	20A / 3.1V	–
10	30A / 2.9V	–
8	40A / 2.5V	–
6	55A / 2.1V	–
4	70A / 1.7V	100A / 2.4V
2	95A / 1.4V	125A / 1.9V
1	–	150A / 1.8V
2/0	–	200A / 1.6V

SWITCHES

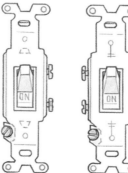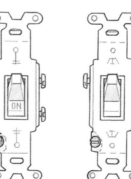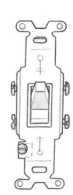

Single-pole   Double-pole   Three-way   Four-way

RUNNING CABLE

Wire the addition with Type NM cable (nonmetallic plastic sheathing), unless codes require a different type.

Staple the cable to framing with approved staples at least every 4½ feet. Cable must also be stapled within 12 inches of metal boxes and within 8 inches of plastic boxes.

When the cable changes direction, bend it no tighter than a radius of five times the cable diameter. Avoid kinks and keep the cable flat, without spirals or twists.

To run cable through framing, drill holes in the centers of the studs or plates so the cable will be at least 1¼ inches from both edges. If it is closer, you must protect the cable from nails and screws with metal plates (available at hardware stores and home centers).

Your local code will specify what kind of cable to run under the floor if it will be exposed. In most areas, NM cable is allowed in crawl spaces, but BX armored cable or UF (Underground Feeder) might be required. Run the cable along the sides of joists and top plates in a basement, or drill holes through the centers of joists.

Don't run cable across the tops of joists in an attic, unless you nail 1× boards on each side as guard strips. You don't have to put guard strips in an attic that has no permanent stairs or ladder, except within 6 feet of the access opening.

Connect cable to metal boxes with approved metal or plastic connectors. Plastic boxes do not require connectors, but you must staple the cable to the framing within 8 inches of the box. Strip the cable sheathing before stapling, leaving about 1 inch of sheathing and 12 inches of wire in the box. Fold the wires back into the box before drywalling to avoid trapping them between the drywall and framing.

Wiring for 3-way and 4-way switches requires cable with three conductors and a ground wire. Cable for these, as well as for ceiling fans, can be 14 gauge (14-3 w/G). The two small appliance circuits for the kitchen can be run with 12-3 w/G cable.

After running cable between all of the boxes and back to the service box (do not connect circuit breaker yet), strip ¾ inch of insulation from the ends of the conductors protruding from the boxes. When white wires act as black wires in switch loops, wrap black electrical tape around them for identification. Do not install the fixtures yet, but make whatever other connections can be made at this time.

Check wiring runs with a continuity tester before having the work inspected and covering it with drywall.

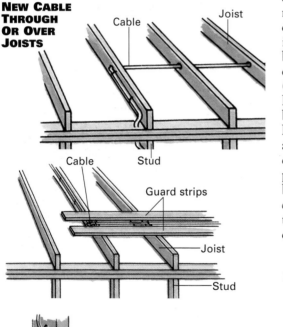

NEW CABLE THROUGH OR OVER JOISTS

Cable — Joist — Cable — Stud

Cable — Guard strips — Joist — Stud

NEW CABLE THROUGH A STUD
A box must extend the thickness of the wall covering beyond the edge of the stud

If the hole is not in the center of the stud, the cable must be protected with a metal plate

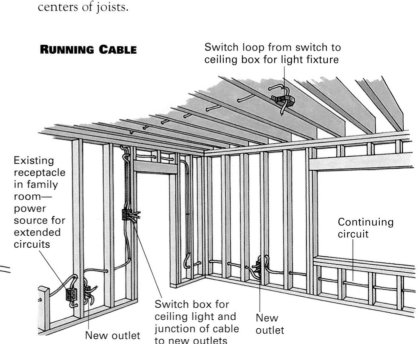

RUNNING CABLE

Switch loop from switch to ceiling box for light fixture

Existing receptacle in family room—power source for extended circuits

Continuing circuit

Switch box for ceiling light and junction of cable to new outlets

New outlet

New outlet

EXTENDING CIRCUITS

You can add fixtures to an existing circuit that is not used to capacity if it is properly wired (grounded, protected by a circuit breaker, and of the correct wire size). Complete the wiring for the circuit extension and turn off the existing circuit before connecting the new wiring to the old.

The easiest place to tap into an existing circuit is at a junction box, usually in the basement, crawl space, or attic. Connect all of the black wires together and all of the white wires together in the box. Connect all of the bare wires together. If the box is metal, connect the bare ground wires to a short pigtail of bare or green wire and connect that wire to a screw or grounding clip in the box. The box must have a metal cover.

TAPPING INTO A JUNCTION BOX

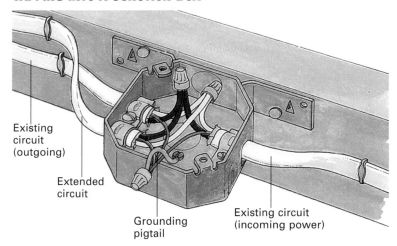

Existing circuit (outgoing)

Extended circuit

Grounding pigtail

Existing circuit (incoming power)

END-OF-RUN RECEPTACLE

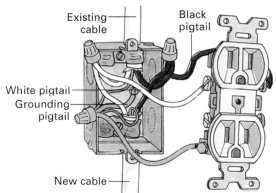

Existing cable

Black pigtail

White pigtail
Grounding pigtail

New cable

WIRING TO AN END-OF-RUN RECEPTACLE

An end-of-run receptacle is a convenient place to add a circuit, as long as the outlet is not controlled by a switch. Run the new cable into the box. Then connect the two black wires to a black pigtail, the two white wires to a white pigtail, and the two bare wires to a bare pigtail. Attach the receptacle to the three pigtails. Include a second bare or green pigtail if grounding a metal box.

WIRING TO A MIDDLE-OF-RUN RECEPTACLE

A middle-of-run box already contains two cables and a receptacle, so you may need a bigger one (see the table, Capacity of Boxes, page 74).

Run the new cable into the box and connect black wires, white wires, and ground wires to their respective pigtails; add another grounding pigtail for a metal box.

WIRING A MIDDLE-OF-RUN SWITCH

If power comes directly to a switch, the box will have two cables entering it, and you can connect a new cable. You cannot tie a new circuit into a switch loop, indicated by a single cable entering the box.

Before turning the power off, turn the switch off and use a voltage tester to find out which black wire is the hot source. Shut off the power and disconnect that wire from the switch. Connect to it the black wire from the new cable and a short black pigtail. Attach the pigtail back to the switch. Connect all bare wires with a pigtail and all white wires without one. Attach the bare pigtail to the switch's green grounding screw.

MIDDLE-OF-RUN SWITCH

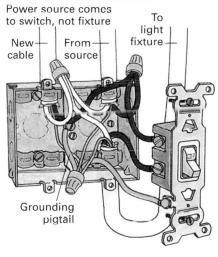

Power source comes to switch, not fixture

New cable

From source

To light fixture

Grounding pigtail

MIDDLE-OF-RUN RECEPTACLE

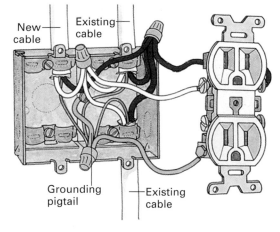

New cable

Existing cable

Grounding pigtail

Existing cable

SWITCH-CONTROLLED CIRCUITS

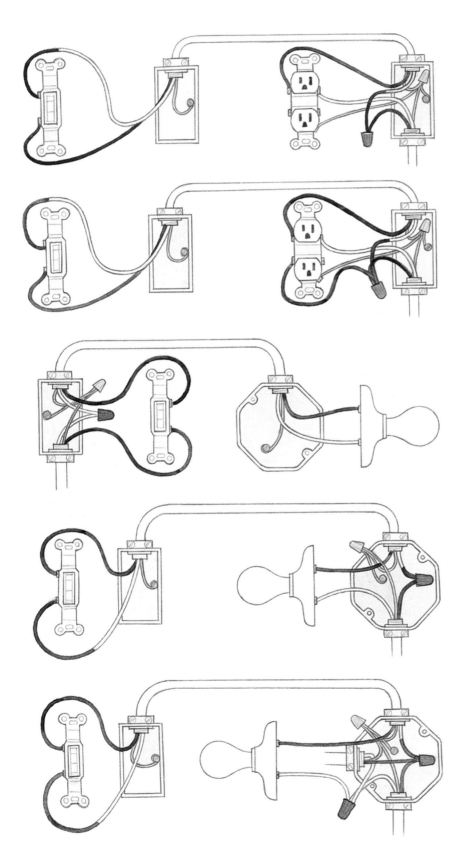

SWITCH-CONTROLLED RECEPTACLE

The black wire feeds through the receptacle box to the switch by way of a white wire marked to designate it as black. The output of the switch feeds back to the receptacle through the black wire.

SPLIT-CIRCUIT RECEPTACLE

This is the same circuit as above, except that the hot jumper tab between the receptacles is removed, so one outlet is switched while the other is always on.

LIGHT AT THE END OF A CIRCUIT

The white wire feeds through the switch box to the light fixture. The black wire (and the power to the light) is controlled by the single-pole switch.

SWITCH AT THE END OF A CIRCUIT

Here the positions of light and switch are reversed. The white wire terminates at the light, while a black/white pair continue to the switch. Because the white wire is being used as a black wire, its ends must be painted or taped black.

LIGHT IN THE MIDDLE OF A CIRCUIT

This is the same circuit as above, except that a third, unswitched cable continues on to a farther box. The black and white wires for this cable are connected to the incoming black and white wires with wire nuts.

3-WAY SWITCHES BEYOND A LIGHT

The black wire continues through the fixture as a black-painted white wire to the common terminal of the first 3-way switch. A red and white pair serves as the traveller (connecting) wires between the two switches. The black wire from the common terminal of the last switch feeds the light. Note that the white traveller wire is marked with black because it is sometimes hot.

LIGHT BETWEEN 3-WAY SWITCHES

The black wire from the source connects to the common terminal of the first switch. The black wire from the common terminal of the second switch feeds the light. The traveller wires connect the matching terminals of the two switches through the fixture box. The red traveller is red all the way; the other traveller is a white wire painted black.

LIGHT BEYOND 3-WAY SWITCHES

Again, the black wire from the source connects to the common terminal of the first switch. The black wire from the common terminal of the second switch feeds the light. The black and red pair between the switches are the travellers.

3- AND 4-WAY SWITCHES

The black wire feeds through the fixture box to the common terminal of the first 3-way switch. A black wire feeds from the common terminal of the second 3-way switch to the light, using one section of white wire designated black. Both sets of red and white travellers from the 3-way switches connect to the equivalent terminals of the 4-way switch in the middle.

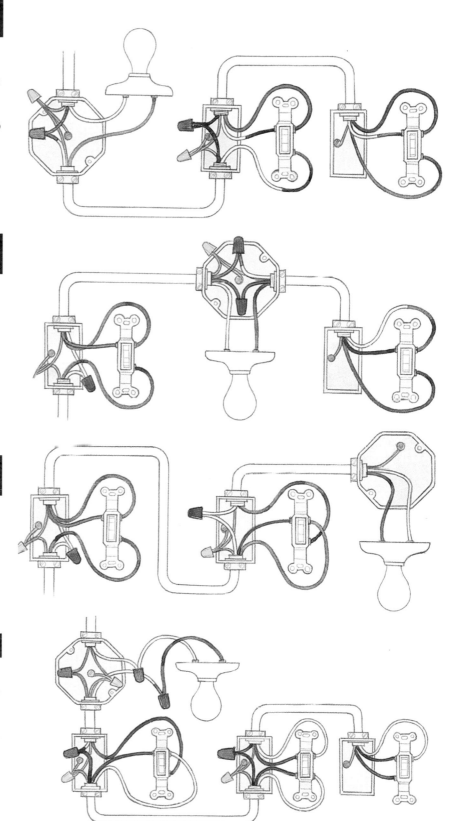

INSULATION

Insulate after the frame and the rough wiring have been inspected. (You may have already insulated under the subfloor.) The plans may specify the required R-values and type of insulation, usually blankets or batts. Besides R-value, there are two other factors that affect insulation performance:

■ Careful installation is important because gaps in the insulation allow heat and air to pass through. Significant heat can escape through a small opening.

■ The warm side of the insulation must be less permeable to moisture than the cold. It might seem dry in winter, but there is more moisture inside a house than outdoors. If this moisture migrates through the insulation to the cold side, it will condense on the sheathing and eventually rot it and the adjacent framing. You should always use insulation with an integral vapor barrier, or install a separate polyethylene plastic vapor barrier over the insulation on the warm side.

Install insulation according to manufacturer's recommendations. Wear a dust mask, goggles, and gloves for protection against irritating fibers. Cut insulation with a utility knife, changing the blade often. Compress thick insulation with a board or carpenter's square to make cutting easier.

ATTIC FLOORS

Since your construction is new, the ceiling joist spacing will be either 16 or 24 inches on-center. Fiberglass blanket (long rolls) and batt (8-foot lengths) are made to fit these joist spacings perfectly. Make sure the vapor barrier faces the warm side (down). Many energy codes call for R-38 or R-49 attic insulation. This is equivalent to 12 or 15 inches of insulation. If you lay two thicknesses of fiberglass, the second layer should be unfaced.

OUTSIDE WALLS

It's convenient to staple kraft- or foil-faced fiberglass between studs, but the facing prevents you from seeing any heat-robbing gaps. It is better to install thick friction-fit batts between the studs, then cover the inside of the wall with 4-mil polyethylene sheeting. When you come to wiring, split the batt, and stuff half behind the cable and half in front of it. Slit an X in the sheeting across switch and electrical boxes, and tape the sheeting to the box before installing drywall.

Cut window openings in the sheeting after the drywall is in place so that the sheeting is trapped between the window rough-opening frame and the drywall.

INSTALLING INSULATION IN AN ATTIC

Vapor barrier

INSTALLING INSULATION IN A WALL

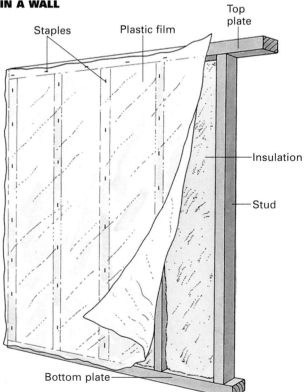

Staples

Plastic film

Top plate

Insulation

Stud

Bottom plate

Molded ventilating channels

CATHEDRAL CEILINGS

Insulating a cathedral ceiling is similar to insulating an exterior wall except for one consideration: ice dams. To prevent meltwater from running down the roof and freezing when it gets to the cold eaves, the roof temperature must be constant from the eaves to the ridge. Channeling cold outside air between the insulation and the roof sheathing solves this problem.

Staple molded-foam ventilating channels to the underside of the roof sheathing before installing the insulation. Vents in the soffit or fascia and a continuous ridge vent serve as air inlets and outlets.

After the vent strips are in place, stuff friction-fit batts between the rafters and cover them with a continuous polyethylene vapor barrier, as shown on the facing page for walls. Or, you can staple the flanges of faced fiberglass batts to the rafter edges, as shown in the illustration at right. This technique works better in roofs than in walls because there is no wiring to cause gaps.

Your energy code may require a higher roof R-value than you can achieve with just fiberglass. If so, install 4x8-foot sheets of rigid foam to the rafter edges or to 1x3 strapping running the other way. The foam provides an additional vapor barrier, but it must be covered with drywall at least ½ inch thick as a fire barrier.

UNDER FLOORS

Many people believe that the earth warms a basement. Although a basement might be warmer than the outdoors on a cold and windy winter day, it is usually not as warm as the rest of the house. Insulating under the floor can reduce heat loss from the upstairs to the basement or crawl space.

Insulating under a floor is the same as insulating a wall or attic: A vapor barrier must be placed on the warm side—this time the top—and ventilation must be provided on the other side.

If your floor sheathing is either plywood or oriented-strand board, and you have glued the tongue-and-groove panel edges, the

waterproof glue in the panels serves as an adequate vapor barrier.

The question is how to hold up the insulation against the relentless force of gravity. The illustration below shows one possibility. Cut rigid panels of molded polystyrene to fit between the joists, then support them with battens screwed to the bottoms of the joists. Molded polystyrene does not act as a vapor barrier because the panels are porous.

You could hold insulation with panels of lauan plywood drilled with occasional 1-inch vent holes. Chicken wire would work, or you could staple a zigzag of monofilament fishing line or nylon cord to the joist bottoms.

Panels work best when there are animals or a lot of air flow under the building; the wire and string are best where the basement or crawl space is closed off.

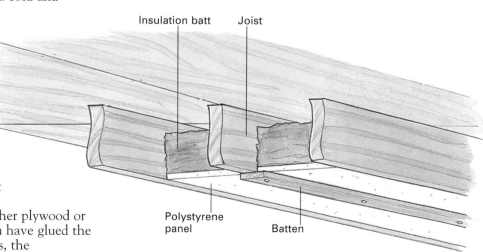

Insulation batt   Joist

Polystyrene panel   Batten

WALLBOARD

Wallboard—also called drywall—isn't difficult to install, but installing it can be messy, dusty, heavy work, especially on a ceiling. An experienced drywaller can measure, cut, and install wallboard at least four times as fast as a novice, so many do-it-yourselfers hire a professional to hang and finish wallboard. If you want the satisfaction of doing it yourself, however, here is how to do it.

PREPARING TO INSTALL WALLBOARD

Plan your layout in advance so you can estimate accurately. Consider using long panels, such as 10-, 12-, or even 14-foot sizes (they're all 4 feet wide), to reduce the number of seams. Drywall panels should run perpendicular to wall studs and ceiling joists. Use full sheets around the tops of windows and doors to eliminate joints that line up with corners—joints there might crack.

Unless your framing lumber is very dry, it may shrink after the wallboard is installed, causing drywall nails to pop out of the surface. Using kiln-dried lumber for framing helps minimize nail popping; so does closing the doors and windows and keeping the room at about 72 degrees F for a week or two before nailing up wallboard. When framing lumber has a high moisture content, install the drywall over dry 1×3 strapping nailed to the studs 16 inches on-center.

If you will install the drywall immediately, stack the sheets upright against the last wall you plan to cover, giving you maximum floor space to work in. If there will be a delay in installation, stack the sheets flat on the floor or they may sag eventually.

Make sure the wall and ceiling framing are straight. Plane down high spots on bowed or twisted studs. Double straight stock next to studs that bow inward. Install blocking where needed to support the panel edges.

Make sure all electrical boxes are mounted so faces will be flush with the finish wall. Wiring that runs through the framing should be at least 1¼ inches from the face of a stud or joist. If not, install an 18-gauge metal protector on the stud or joist edge.

ESTIMATING WALLBOARD SUPPLIES

To estimate the number of wallboard sheets you'll need, refer to the illustration on the opposite page and follow these steps (the estimate assumes an 8-foot-tall wall, using 4×8 sheets):
1. Measure the room perimeter in feet.
2. Divide the measurement by 4; round up to the nearest whole number.
3. Deduct the following amounts:
   for each door—⅓ sheet
   for each window—¼ sheet
   for a bay window or patio door—⅔ sheet
   for a bookcase or fireplace—½ sheet
4. Round the result up to a whole sheet.
5. To estimate the number of sheets for the ceiling, divide the width of the room by 4 and divide the length of the room by 8; round both answers up, then multiply them together to find the number of sheets.

After figuring the total number of sheets, determine the right amount of ready-mix joint compound, joint tape, and fasteners by following the line across from the number of whole sheets on the chart below.

Drywall is also available in lengths of 10, 12, and 14 feet. If you are using sheets larger than 4×8, increase the amounts of the supplies proportional to the increased area.

ESTIMATING WALLBOARD SUPPLIES

Drywall, 4×8 Sheets	Compound, gallons	Joint Tape, feet	Screws, pounds		or	Nails, pounds	
			1¼"	⅝"		1¼"	1⅝"
8	2	95	0.8	1.0		1.0	1.4
10	2	118	1.0	1.3		1.3	1.7
12	3	142	1.2	1.6		1.5	2.0
16	4	190	1.6	2.1		2.0	2.7
20	4	237	2.0	2.6		2.6	3.4
24	5	285	2.5	3.1		3.1	4.1

INSTALLING CEILING PANELS

Mark the centers of all ceiling joists on the wall plates so you will know where to nail after the panels are up. Then, starting along one wall, lift the first panel into place and attach it to the joists with 1¼-inch ringshank wallboard nails or wallboard screws. Begin fastening at the center of the panel and work outward. Space nails 7 inches apart, screws 12 inches apart. Nails and screws should be at least ⅜ inch from the panel edge. Drive them in until they sink slightly into the paper covering (dimpling it without ripping it) so the joint compound can easily cover the heads.

Measure, cut to fit, and install the remaining panels. Stagger all end joints at least one joist spacing—don't line up end joints all across the room. If you cut the edge or end off any panels, place the fresh cut against the wall, leaving a slight gap. Join the factory-beveled edge of the panel against the beveled edges of other panels. This makes joint taping easier.

If there are any electrical fixtures, flues, or other obstructions in the ceiling, measure and mark the hole locations carefully and cut them out with a wallboard saw (see page 84). Gaps around ceiling boxes and other obstructions should be no larger than ¼ inch.

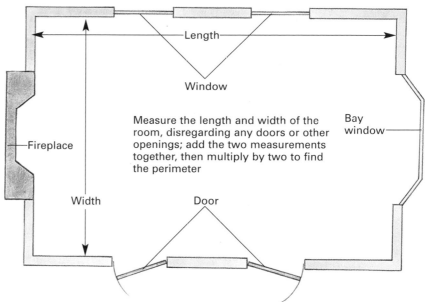

Measure the length and width of the room, disregarding any doors or other openings; add the two measurements together, then multiply by two to find the perimeter

apart. Snap chalk lines on the wallboard between the marks on the ceiling and floor to show where the centers of the studs are for nailing.

TAPING AND FINISHING

Before covering the fasteners or joints, check with the building inspector—you might have to have an inspection. After that, tape and finish the drywall as shown on page 85.

INSTALLING WALL PANELS

Mark the centers of all studs on both ceiling and floor. If you are installing the panels horizontally—which is recommended—place the top panel first so you can snug it up against the ceiling. Then snug the bottom panel up against the top panel, and fill any gaps under it with narrow strips of wallboard. (These do not have to be finished if they will be covered by a baseboard.)

Attach panels with screws or nails that penetrate the framing at least ¾ inch. Cut the panels with enough clearance so you don't have to force them into place. Space nails 8 inches apart, screws 12 inches

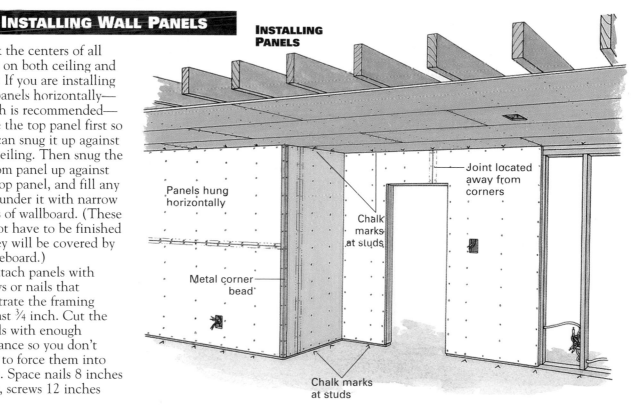

INSTALLING PANELS

Joint located away from corners

Panels hung horizontally

Chalk marks at studs

Metal corner bead

Chalk marks at studs

WALLBOARD
continued

MARKING AND CUTTING

After marking a straight cut, cut through the paper face of the good side, using a utility knife and a straightedge.

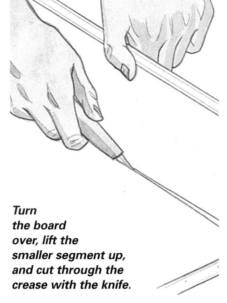

Turn the board over, lift the smaller segment up, and cut through the crease with the knife.

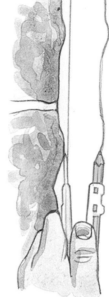

To mark an irregular cut, set a child's drawing compass to about 1 inch and trace the shape while holding the compass legs horizontal.

To cut a notch, make the long cut with the utility knife and the short cut with a wallboard saw. Then fold the board back along the long cut, and cut the back side with the knife.

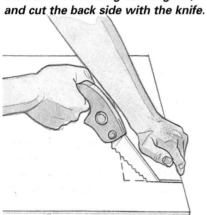

One way to cut a rectangular hole, such as one for a receptacle box, is with a wallboard saw. First mark the outline of the hole.

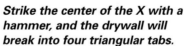

Then push the sharp tip of the saw through the wallboard at one corner and saw along the line. Punch and saw through remaining sides.

Another way to make holes is to cut through the paper on all four sides, then diagonally with an X.

Strike the center of the X with a hammer, and the drywall will break into four triangular tabs.

Turn the board over, raise the tabs, and cut along the creases to remove the tabs.

TAPING AND FINISHING SEAMS

1. Spread a layer of compound along the entire length of a joint

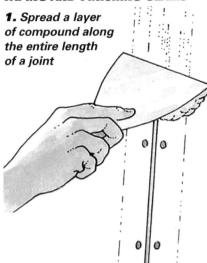

2. Lay tape into wet compound and smooth with a 3" or 4" putty knife. Wetting the tape keeps it from binding

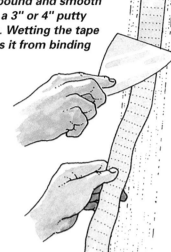

3. With a 4" knife, apply a thin layer of compound. Feather the edges carefully

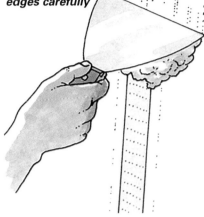

4. Fill and smooth all dimples with a layer of compound

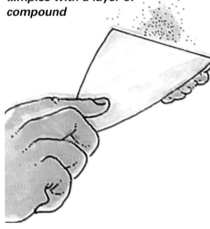

5. Let compound dry thoroughly, then sand. Or, moisten the compound with a wet sponge and smooth it with a 4" knife

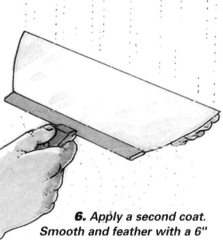

6. Apply a second coat. Smooth and feather with a 6" knife. Sand when dry. Apply a third coat and sand lightly when dry

OUTSIDE CORNERS

1. Nail on a metal corner strip, making sure the fit is smooth and tight

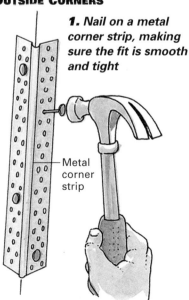

Metal corner strip

2. Apply compound with a putty knife or a corner trowel

3. Finish as for a taped joint

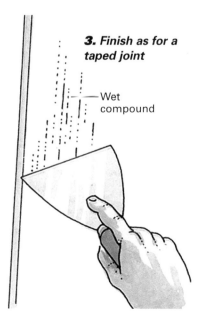

Wet compound

Make several passes with a utility knife and straightedge to get the exact fit. Make the first one within ½ inch, the next within ⅛ inch. Leave a ⅛-inch gap for expansion.

Cut along the center of the overlap, using a straightedge as a guide. Press hard enough to cut cleanly through both layers. Remove any scrap or dirt from under the seam.

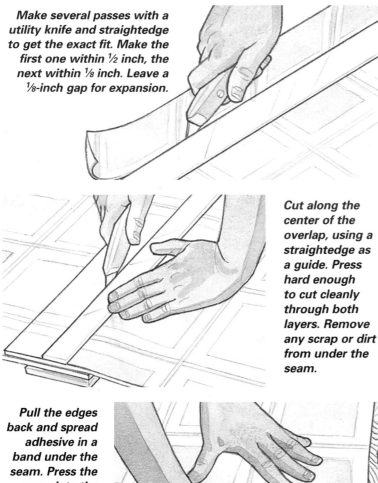

Pull the edges back and spread adhesive in a band under the seam. Press the seam into the adhesive and wipe up any that squeezes out. Clean the surface immediately.

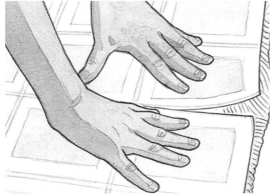

After several hours, apply seam sealer to the edges with the applicator tip. The sealer fuses the vinyl together to make a waterproof joint.

FLOORING

SHEET VINYL

Install a 5/16-inch underlayment of lauan plywood or hardboard over the subfloor. Nail with 2d ringshank nails, 4 inches on center. Leave a 1/16- to 1/8-inch gap between the panels for expansion. Fill all gaps, holes, cracks, and nail depressions with a durable, fast-drying compound.

Sheet vinyl must be cut accurately, whether it's laid loose as a full sheet or adhered at the seams. The easiest way to fit the sheet is to make a preliminary paper pattern. Tape large pieces of kraft paper together, and trim the pattern to fit the floor. Work carefully to make a precise pattern.

The resilient sheet, which comes in 6- and 12-foot widths, should be unrolled and allowed to relax at room temperature for several hours before cutting. If you have to seam two pieces of vinyl, tape them together with a 2-inch overlap at the seam. Then lay the paper pattern over the vinyl, tape it down, and cut, allowing an extra inch at all margins.

Lay the vinyl in place, making sure that the margins curl up against the wall, and follow the illustrations at left.

PREFINISHED FLOORS

FLOATING FLOOR: Prefinished flooring consists of strips of medium-density fiberboard (MDF) finished on both sides with plastic laminate. The strips are precisely machined with tongue-and-groove edges. The floating installation is easy to do:
1. Cover the floor with ⅛-inch foam pad.
2. Dry-lay a row of planks across the room. If the last plank will be narrower than 2 inches, rip the first plank to adjust it.
3. Lay the planks, leaving a ⅜-inch gap along each wall. Insert spacers between the flooring and the wall.
4. As you lay each plank, run a bead of carpenter's glue inside its groove. Tap the plank into place, using a piece of scrap flooring as shown below.
5. Wipe off excess glue immediately.

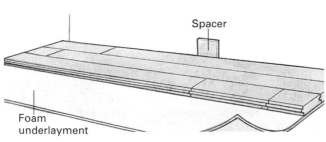

Spacer

Foam underlayment

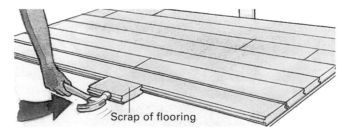

Scrap of flooring

Before gluing any strips down, lay the flooring in a test pattern to see how the pieces fall at doors and corners. Adjust the layout so you have no strip narrower than 2 inches.

You can test-fit quickly and easily on a computer with drawing software. Measure the room exactly and draw it to scale on the computer. Assemble several strips of flooring and measure the net width exactly. Create strips to the same scale, snap them together, and try different arrangements on the computer screen until you get the best fit.

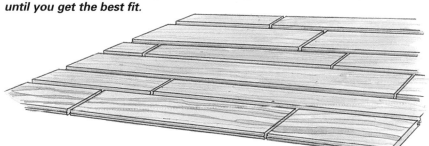

Cut strips to length with a power miter saw or a backsaw and a miter box. Make other cuts with a jigsaw or table saw, as appropriate. When using a jigsaw, clamp the strip firmly with cardboard under the clamp to protect the finish.

FASTENED-DOWN FLOOR: Gluing the strips to the subfloor takes more work, but results in a more solid-feeling floor. When deciding whether to glue, consider the expected lifetime of the floor. Prefinished MDF flooring cannot be sanded the way a floor of solid-hardwood strips can. Glued-down prefinished flooring is not a good choice for high-traffic areas because replacing strips that have worn or damaged finish would be difficult. If you decide to glue the floor down, here is how to do it:

1. Carefully remove and save all of the baseboards; they will cover the edges of the new flooring.

2. Remove any existing flooring, such as vinyl tile, sheet vinyl, or carpeting, down to the subfloor.

3. Repair any damage to the subfloor. Make sure the subfloor is sound, smooth, and level.

4. Measure the thickness of the new flooring, and cut the bottoms of door casings so the planks will slip under.

5. Break the flooring bundles, and spread the planks around in the room for several days so that they reach moisture equilibrium.

6. Follow the steps illustrated below to install the flooring.

Make paper templates for complex cuts, such as in doorways and around pipes. Trim the template carefully, then transfer its outline onto the flooring. Cut along the outline with a jigsaw.

Test-fit a strip that has a complex cut and adjust the fit as necessary. Then place the strip and mark its edge on the subfloor as a guideline for the adhesive. Apply the adhesive to the subfloor.

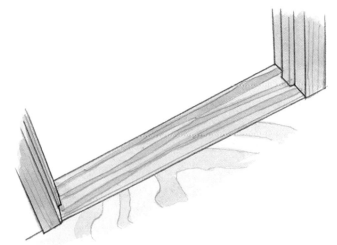

Place the strip; keep sliding to a minimum (too much sliding might push the adhesive ahead and out of the joint). Tap the piece into place and press it into the subfloor evenly.

FLOORING
continued

TONGUE-AND-GROOVE HARDWOOD STRIP FLOORING

Traditional ¾-inch, tongue-and-groove, hardwood strip flooring takes the most work to install but results in a solid, durable floor. Nails don't show because the tongue is covered by the groove of the next board, and the material is thick enough to sand and refinish many times. Oak and maple are the most popular hardwood floors.

PREPARATIONS

The flooring is usually dry when shipped. Acclimatize the strips by opening the bundles and spreading the strips around the space you will be flooring. Let them sit for at least five days at about 70 degrees F. The flooring might add moisture to the air, so have the drywall taping and painting complete.

Remove the baseboards carefully so you can reuse them, and cut the bottoms of door casings so the flooring will just slip under them. As you remove the baseboards, write on the back of each piece where it came from.

If flooring a kitchen, decide whether to install flooring under a built-in dishwasher or to place the machine directly on the subfloor. Measure the washer and countertop heights carefully to make sure the appliance will fit before you install flooring under it. Don't trap equipment under a counter by flooring up to the front of it, either.

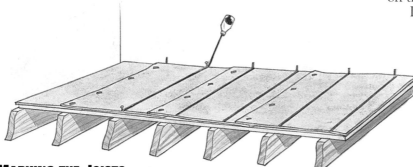

MARKING THE JOISTS

Unless there is good reason not to, lay strip flooring perpendicular to the joists. Nails in the subfloor will help you locate the joist centers. Line up a string over the nails, and mark the joist centers on the walls. If the floor is not over a heated space, cover it with 15-pound felt.
Lay the strips parallel to the joists, overlapped 4 inches and stapled to the subfloor. Using the marks on the walls, snap chalk lines over the joist centers.

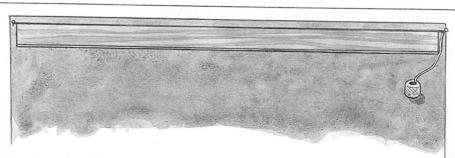

THE STARTER STRIP

Snap a chalk line ¾ inch out from the wall. Lay the first strip down with its grooved edge along the chalk line and its end ½ inch from the right-end wall. Face-nail it at every joist with a pair of 8d finish nails. If the flooring is oak or maple, predrill the holes to avoid splitting the strip. Finish the row ½ inch from the left end, and use the remainder to start the next row.

NAILING

Toenail the next few courses by hand until there is enough room to use a floor nailing machine. Drive *8d finish nails at 45 degrees just above the tongue, and set the heads with a nail set, being careful not to mar the finish. Both by hand* *and with the nailing machine, drive nails at every joist (on the chalk line), halfway between, and 2 inches from the end of every piece.*

PLANNING

If the floor is a simple rectangle, start ¾ inch from one of the long walls and lay parallel strips until you reach the opposite wall. Place the first strip with the groove toward the wall so that the tongue is always exposed for nailing.

If the flooring will extend into other rooms, plan ahead to keep the tongue edge exposed as you work. You might have to reverse the direction of the tongue by inserting a spline into a groove, converting the groove into a tongue. Most flooring suppliers stock matching splines for this purpose.

NAILING MACHINE

A nailing machine drives finish nails or staples at the correct angle and location on the tongue for blind nailing. The heavy mallet ensures that a single blow will set the nail all the way.

Air-powered flooring nailers are lighter. Because compressed air does the driving, they are easier to use. Most drive flooring staples instead of nails.

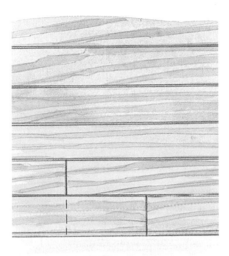

RANDOM PATTERN

For both strength and appearance, joints should be staggered. For a random pattern, mix long and short pieces, and always start a course with the cutoff piece from the previous course. As you go, check each piece to make sure its end will fall at least 6 inches from a joint in the previous course. Stack random-length flooring according to length so you can keep track of what's left.

THE LAST STRIP

There won't be room for the nailing machine on the last rows. When you can no longer use the machine, fasten the remaining strips by hand. The last strip will probably have to be ripped to width; be sure to cut off the tongue side. Use a piece of scrap wood to protect the wall as you pry the last strip into place. Predrill the strip to prevent splitting, then face-nail it.

BOARD FEET OF HARDWOOD STRIP FLOORING
(ASSUMES 5 PERCENT WASTE)

Floor Area, square feet	Size, inches						
	¾×1½	¾×2¼	¾×3¼	½×1½	½×2	⅜×1½	⅜×2
5	8	7	6	7	7	7	7
10	16	14	13	14	13	14	13
20	31	28	26	28	26	28	26
30	47	42	39	42	39	42	39
40	62	55	52	55	52	55	52
50	78	69	65	69	65	69	65
60	93	83	77	83	78	83	78
70	109	97	90	97	91	97	91
80	124	111	103	111	104	111	104
90	140	125	116	125	117	125	117
100	155	138	129	138	130	138	130

FLOORING
continued

CARPET

Installing carpet over a pad doesn't require much preparation. Remove the old carpet, the old pad, and the tackless strip around the edge of the room. Go over the floor carefully and remove any nails or staples.

The instructions below are for installing carpet over a wood subfloor. If the floor is a concrete slab, you will have to nail the tackless strip around the edge with concrete nails. Before doing that, make sure the slab does not contain any radiant-heat pipes that you might puncture when nailing.

If there are radiant-heat pipes, wet the floor, then turn up the heat. The areas that dry first will reveal locations of the pipes. Mark them with a felt marker or chalk.

After you install the tackless strip, install the carpet pad, following the instructions accompanying the illustration below. Then, rough-fit the carpet. Seam it and fit it to the room, as shown in the illustrations on the opposite page.

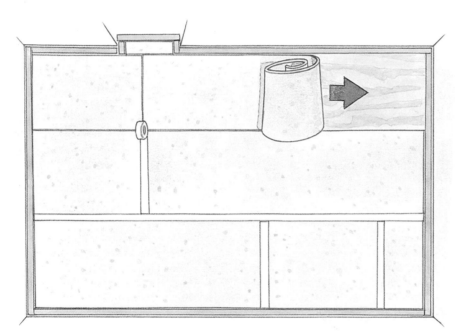

Installing Carpet Pad
First, nail the tackless strip (available from carpet dealers) around the perimeter of the room, leaving a space of two-thirds the carpet thickness between the strip and the wall. The teeth should point toward the wall. Substitute gripper edge (see illustration on the facing page) for tackless strip at doorways or other open areas.

Cut and fit sections of carpet pad to fit inside the tackless strip. Staple down the edge of the pad every 6 inches, leaving a ½-inch gap between the pad and the tackless strip. Cover the seams between the sections of pad with duct tape.

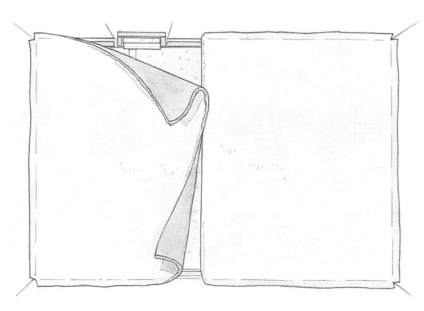

Rough-Fitting the Carpet
Make a sketch of the sizes of the carpet pieces you need, then cut each piece from the roll, allowing an extra 4 inches in length and width for trimming. Make sure when cutting and placing the pieces that the pile goes the same way.

Except for loop-pile, always cut carpet from the back side so that the yarns are not cut. Use a utility knife with a fresh blade.

After the pieces are cut, place them so they curl up the walls and overlap by at least 1 inch at the seams. Slit the folded-up corners so the carpet will lie flat.

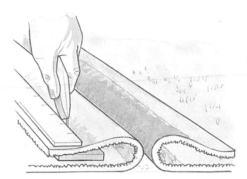

Cutting the Seam
Measure equal distances from where folded pieces meet and snap chalk lines on both sides. Cut along the chalk lines with a sharp utility knife, using a straightedge and a backing board.

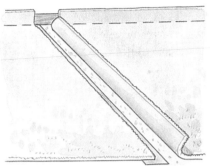

Seaming Tape
After adjusting the pieces so that they butt perfectly, cut a piece of hot-melt seaming tape to length and center it under the seam with the adhesive side facing up.

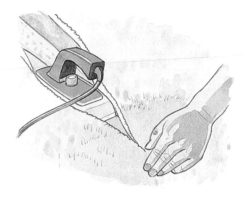

Heating the Seam
Starting at one end, slide a seaming iron (you can rent one from the carpet dealer) slowly along the seam and pinch the seam together. Have someone walk on the seam to press it down as you heat it.

The Knee Kicker
Following the sequence shown in the diagrams at right, stretch and kick the carpet into place. To work the kicker, press its head into the

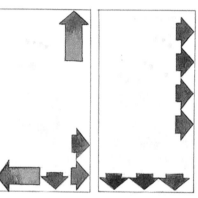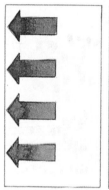

carpet about 1 inch from the wall. Then, while still pressing down, give the knee pad a swift kick with your knee. The teeth of the tackless strip should hook the carpet.

For large rooms, rent a power stretcher to use where indicated by the long arrows. Ask for instructions when you rent the stretcher.

Trimming
Adjust the wall trimmer for the carpet thickness. Press the trimmer against both the wall and floor, and slice off the excess carpet. Trim the areas the trimmer can't reach with a utility knife.

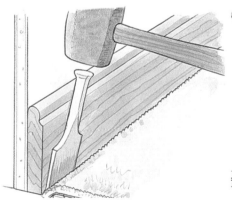

Tucking the Edges
Force the edge of the carpet into the gap between the wall and the tackless strip. If you have removed the baseboard and plan to replace it, this tucking step is not necessary.

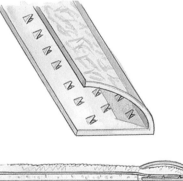

Door Openings
At doorways and other wall openings, trim and press the carpet edge into the gripper strip. Using a wood scrap to protect the strip, pound it down over the carpet to clamp it.

INTERIOR TRIM

Interior trim includes baseboards and casings for the windows and doors. There may also be other trim to install, such as crown molding at the ceiling, but the techniques are similar.

To install trim, you'll need a 16-ounce finish hammer, nail set, fine-toothed backsaw, miter box, bevel gauge, and try square. You can also use a power miter saw or a sliding compound miter saw to make the cuts.

It's usually best to finish painting or wallpapering the walls before you install the trim. It also saves a lot of time and mess if you prepaint the trim itself before cutting and installing it.

DOOR CASINGS

Casings should not be flush with the inside edge of jambs but should be set back about ¼ inch to reveal some of the jamb. This setback distance is called the reveal. Mark it on the edges of the jambs.

To install the casing, square one end of a piece of casing. Stand it on the floor and align its inside edge along the left reveal. Mark it at the top where the reveal lines intersect, as shown below left.

At this mark, cut the casing at 45 degrees and nail it in place with 4d finish nails at the jamb edge and 6d finish nails into the studs.

Cut the left end of the head (top) casing at a 45-degree angle, and hold it in place. Mark its bottom edge where the reveal lines intersect on the right jamb and make a 45-degree cut outward from the mark. Tack the head casing in place.

Square an end of a third piece of casing and stand it in place. Mark both inside and outside edges where they cross the mitered head casing. Scribe the casing between the marks, make the miter cut, and nail the casing to the jamb and wall.

INSTALLING A MITERED DOOR CASING

Rabbet

Mark the reveal, a ¼" space between frame and casing

¼"

Door jamb

Follow this procedure to measure and mark mitered door casings.

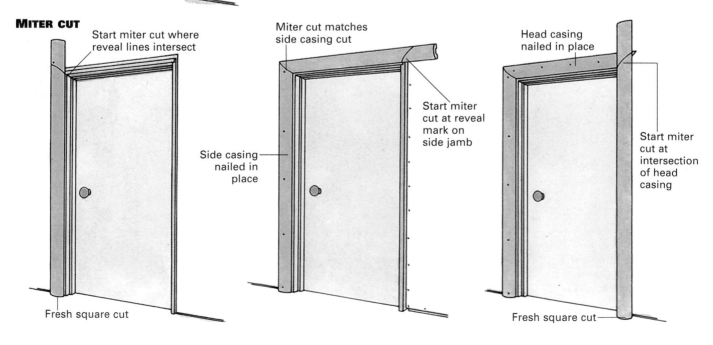

MITER CUT

Start miter cut where reveal lines intersect

Fresh square cut

Miter cut matches side casing cut

Side casing nailed in place

Start miter cut at reveal mark on side jamb

Head casing nailed in place

Start miter cut at intersection of head casing

Fresh square cut

WINDOW CASINGS

Measure and cut the stool—the interior windowsill. The stool fits against the bottom window sash between the jambs, and the ends are cut to make horns that extend ¼ inch beyond each side casing. Install mitered side and head casings as described on the facing page for doors. Complete the window trim with an apron under the stool. The apron ends align with the outside edges of the casings.

The illustration at far right shows mitered-corner trim and three other corner styles. The two butted joints at the top are the most common. Rosette blocks, as shown in the lower right example, can be ordered at a lumberyard.

PARTS OF A WINDOW

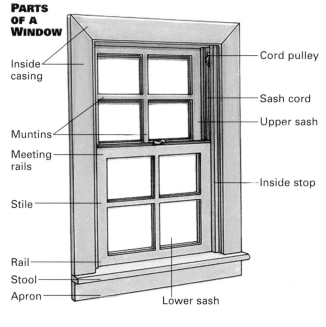

Inside casing

Cord pulley

Sash cord

Upper sash

Muntins

Meeting rails

Inside stop

Stile

Rail

Stool

Apron

Lower sash

1-PIECE BASEBOARD

BASEBOARDS

Baseboards can be made up of one, two, or three pieces of standard molding. Leave a ½-inch gap beneath the baseboard for the floor covering if it is not already in place. If you are installing a base shoe against the bottom of the baseboard, install it after the finish flooring.

Use miter cuts to join baseboards at outside corners. At inside corners, use a butt joint for square-edged stock and a coped joint for moldings.

2-PIECE BASEBOARD

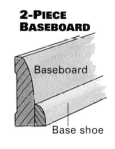

Baseboard

Base shoe

3-PIECE BASEBOARD

Base cap

Baseboard

Base shoe

INSTALLING BASEBOARDS

For a coped joint, square the end of the first piece of baseboard and install it. Cut the second piece at a 45-degree angle.

Then make a second cut along the contour of the first piece, holding the coping saw perpendicular to the board. Fit the second piece of molding over the first piece and nail it in place.

Moldings should be nailed with 8d finish nails through the drywall into the studs. If you need to probe to find the studs, do so at the bottom of the wall where your test holes will be covered by the baseboard.

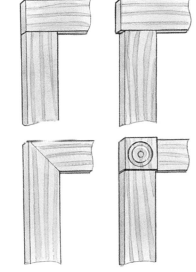

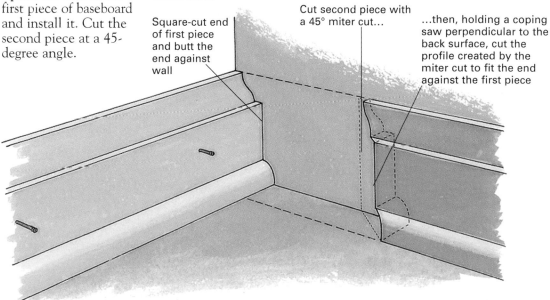

Square-cut end of first piece and butt the end against wall

Cut second piece with a 45° miter cut...

...then, holding a coping saw perpendicular to the back surface, cut the profile created by the miter cut to fit the end against the first piece

KITCHENS AND BATHS

CABINET STYLES

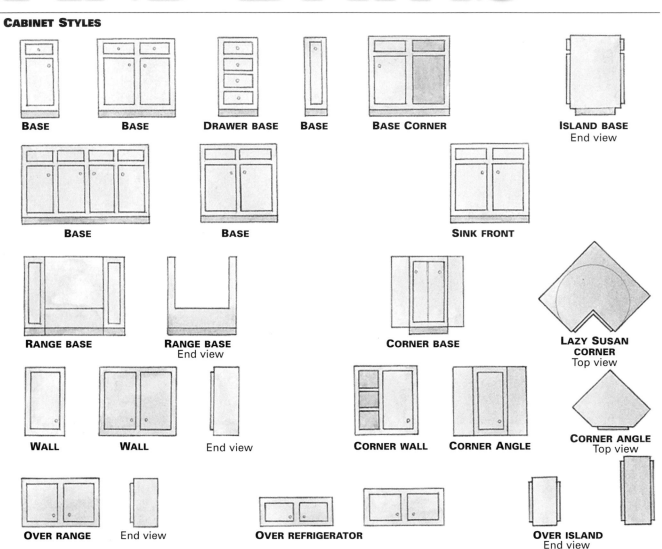

BASE   BASE   DRAWER BASE   BASE   BASE CORNER   ISLAND BASE
End view

BASE   BASE   SINK FRONT

RANGE BASE   RANGE BASE
End view   CORNER BASE   LAZY SUSAN CORNER
Top view

WALL   WALL   End view   CORNER WALL   CORNER ANGLE   CORNER ANGLE
Top view

OVER RANGE   End view   OVER REFRIGERATOR   OVER ISLAND
End view

CABINETS

Preassembled kitchen cabinets and bathroom vanities are available in standard sizes and in a range of quality. Manufactured cabinets are not inexpensive, but they usually cost less than custom cabinets of the same quality.

Although cabinet sizes are fairly standard, not every manufacturer offers all of the possible cabinet configurations. So, before deciding on a detailed kitchen design with exact cabinet sizes, choose a cabinet brand and style. Lumberyards and home centers usually have cabinet samples and many offer free design services.

After choosing a cabinet line, sit down with the kitchen designer and develop a detailed kitchen plan.

Delivery of the cabinets may take anywhere from a few hours to a few months. Check delivery times with the dealer to make sure a lack of cabinets doesn't delay completion of your project.

Some common cabinets styles are shown above. Base and wall cabinets come in a number of lengths to simplify layouts.

KITCHEN PLAN SHOWING CABINETS

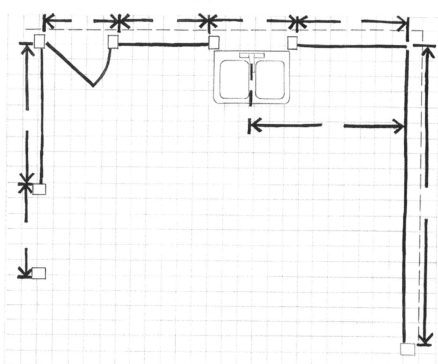

KITCHEN PLAN

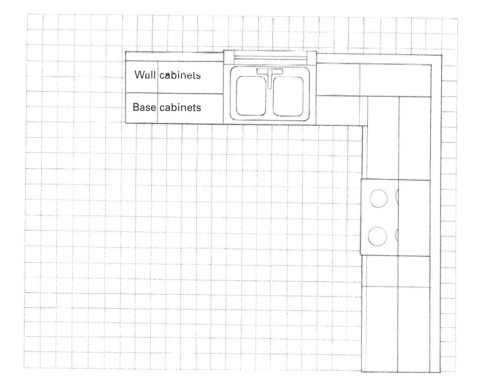

COMPUTER-AIDED DESIGN

Take advantage of free design services at a lumberyard or home center. Here's why:
■ Two heads are better than one, especially when one is a professional in the area.
■ The designer can suggest solutions and produce the final design, but you still have final say.
■ If you give the designer accurate room dimensions, you have some recourse with the dealer if something doesn't fit at installation.

Here are the usual steps in working up a kitchen design:
■ Determine the dimensions of your kitchen. Don't take these dimensions from your plans. Measure the finished walls, trim, and rough-in plumbing to the nearest ⅛ inch. The designer will need to know:
■ wall lengths
■ locations of the outside edges of door and window casings
■ locations of plumbing supply and drain pipes
■ ceiling and windowsill heights
■ appliance dimensions
■ Transfer these dimensions to a piece of graph paper, as shown above right. Draw the layout on graph paper with a grid that has one square equal to 3, 6, or 12 inches. Don't worry about the accuracy of your sketch; the designer will rely on your written dimensions.
■ Visit home centers and lumberyards to chose a cabinet line and style.
■ Go over your sketch with the home center's designer, who will key your dimensions into the computer. Then, as you select cabinets, the computer will put them into place on the plan. You can look at the design in three dimensions from any point in the room. Once the design is final, the computer will print the list of cabinets and prices, then place the order.

ACCESSIBLE KITCHENS

Since enactment of the Americans with Disabilities Act, much research has gone into ways to make public facilities accessible for people in wheelchairs. Use the kitchen guidelines here and the bathroom guidelines on page 103 to make your home more accessible to a family member or guest who uses a wheelchair. You might eventually need a more accessible home yourself if you plan to stay in the home for a long time.

For further details, see the Code of Federal Regulations, 28 CFR, Part 36, Appendix A. It can be found on the Internet or in any large library.

DOORWAYS

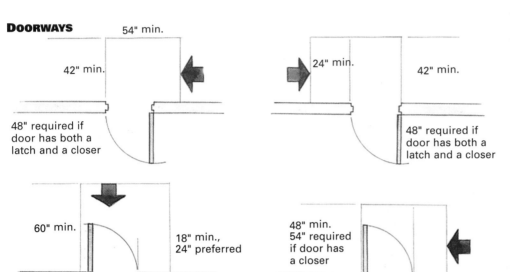

54" min.

42" min.

48" required if door has both a latch and a closer

24" min.

42" min.

48" required if door has both a latch and a closer

60" min.

18" min., 24" preferred

48" min. 54" required if door has a closer

COUNTERS AND RANGES

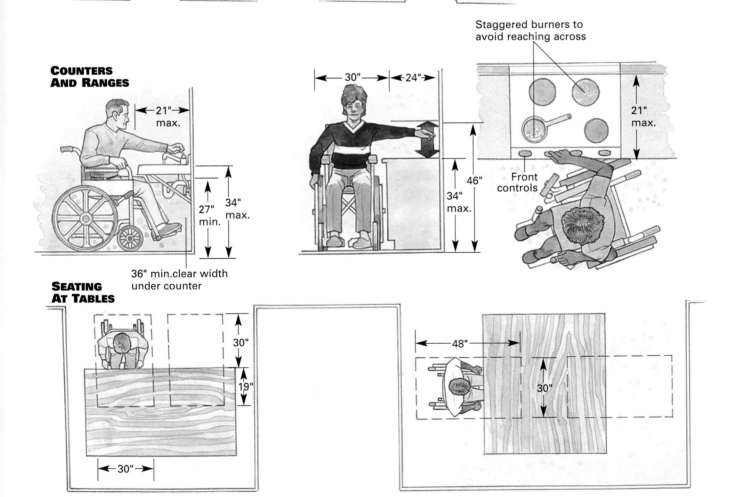

21" max.

27" min.

34" max.

36" min. clear width under counter

30"

24"

46"

34" max.

Staggered burners to avoid reaching across

21" max.

Front controls

SEATING AT TABLES

30"

19"

30"

48"

30"

KITCHEN FRAMING

BLOCKING

To make wall cabinet installation easier, nail blocking (2×10 or 2×12) between studs where the tops of cabinets will be.

WING WALLS AND KNEE WALLS

A short wall can hide a refrigerator, define an alcove, or terminate a countertop. If it is full height, attach its top plates to ceiling joists or into blocking between the joists.

A shorter wall can create a feeling of more space and admit more daylight into an alcove. The wall must be stiffened because it has no support along the top and one edge. You can brace the wall with a corner cabinet, shelving, or a counter installed against the wing wall and the adjacent wall.

Assemble the frame of a freestanding wall with screws instead of nails, and cover it with either ⅝-inch drywall or ½-inch plywood. For maximum strength and rigidity, extend the last stud through the floor and attach it to a joist underneath, as shown at right.

PASS-THROUGHS

Frame a pass-through like a window, with a double rough sill across the bottom and a header at the top. If the pass-through will be in an existing bearing wall, shore up the ceiling joists on each side of the proposed opening before cutting any studs. Rather than removing studs from the opening, cut them off at the height of the pass-through, allowing for the double rough sill and the finish shelf or trim.

SOFFITS

Soffits fill the space between the ceiling and wall cabinets. Soffits are usually framed after covering the walls and ceiling with wallboard. To allow for crooked walls or discrepancies in cabinets, the finished soffit is usually made 1 inch deeper than the cabinets that will hang below it. This creates a narrow overhang just above cabinets, so cover the wallboard with a corner bead along this edge.

Frame the soffit with 2×2s to make it easier to drive nails or screws in both directions. Choose lumber for straightness; warps or bows will show. You can frame the soffit with 2×3s

or 2×4s, which increases rigidity but requires toenailing for assembly.

Build the L-shape ladder frame on the floor, then raise it into place and secure it by nailing or screwing one rail into the ceiling joists and the other into the wall studs. Cover the soffit framing with wallboard.

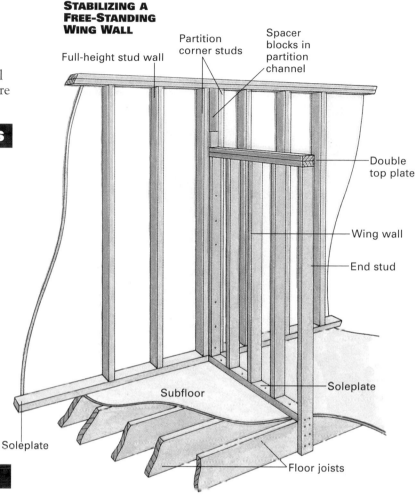

STABILIZING A FREE-STANDING WING WALL

Full-height stud wall — Partition corner studs — Spacer blocks in partition channel — Double top plate — Wing wall — End stud — Soleplate — Subfloor — Soleplate — Floor joists

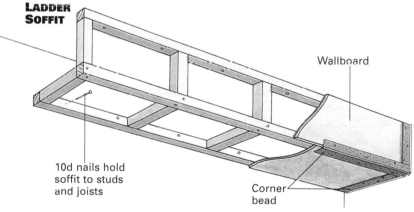

LADDER SOFFIT

Wallboard — 10d nails hold soffit to studs and joists — Corner bead

DRAINPIPES AND VENT PIPES

DRAIN BETWEEN JOISTS

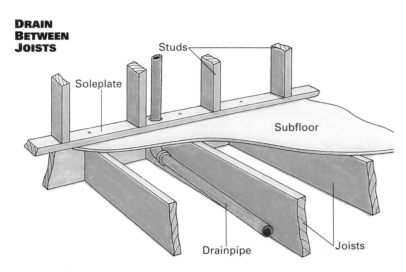

Studs
Soleplate
Subfloor
Drainpipe
Joists

VENT PIPE BELOW KITCHEN WINDOW

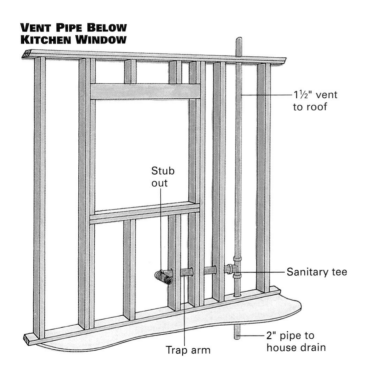

1½" vent to roof
Stub out
Sanitary tee
Trap arm
2" pipe to house drain

VENTING AN ISLAND SINK

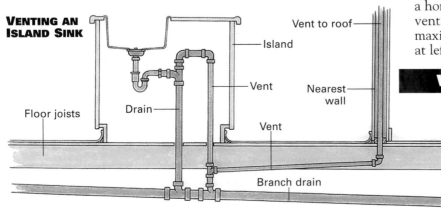

Vent to roof
Island
Vent
Nearest wall
Floor joists
Drain
Vent
Branch drain

D rains are the most difficult aspect of plumbing because they must slope between ⅛ inch and ¼ inch per foot. So, if you extend a drain to a new sink location, there might not be enough clearance to slope it to the new fixture if the existing drain is strapped close to the bottom of the floor joists. A kitchen sink with a dishwasher requires a 2-inch drainpipe. You might be able to run the new pipe parallel to the joists and suspend it between them. It might also be possible to bore through 2×10 or 2×12 joists for a 2-inch pipe (the holes must be at least 2 inches from the joist edges). Otherwise, the drainpipe will have to connect to the main drain farther downstream.

All plumbing fixtures must be vented. Venting allows air to circulate in the drainage system without siphoning water out of traps or applying backpressure to them, which would break the seal. If you install a sink near the old location, you can use the same vent, provided you don't exceed the trap arm distance—the maximum distance between the outlet of the sink trap and the vent pipe. (Distances are normally 3½ feet for 1½-inch drainpipe and 6 feet for 2-inch pipe.)

VENTING A SINK UNDER A WINDOW

Kitchen sinks usually have windows over them so you don't face a wall while working at the sink. The window also makes it impossible to run a vent pipe directly to the roof next to the sink. Codes prohibit changing a vent pipe direction from vertical to horizontal lower than 42 inches above the floor, which is higher than most windowsills. But you can offset the vent pipe to clear the window with two 45-degree fittings, avoiding a 90-degree change in direction below the 42-inch limit. Or, you can place a vertical vent pipe alongside the window and run a horizontal trap arm from the sink to the vent, as long as it does not exceed the maximum trap arm distance, as shown at left center.

VENTING AN ISLAND SINK

Venting an island sink without installing a vent pipe through the middle of the room is a problem similar to venting a sink with a window over it. Most codes accept the venting arrangement shown in the illustration at left.

WATER SUPPLY PIPES

Run the supply pipes after the drain and vent pipes. A dishwasher requires a ⅜-inch supply, usually flexible copper tubing, connected to an angle stop under the sink or dishwasher. A refrigerator with an icemaker requires its own cold water supply—typically ⅜-inch tubing with a separate angle stop behind or next to the refrigerator.

ROUGH-IN DIMENSIONS

Kitchen sink rough-in dimensions are usually 15 inches above the floor for the drain stub and 19 inches for supply stubs. If the sink is against an outside wall in a northern climate, however, you should run the supply pipes up through the floor to prevent freezing.

FREEZE PROTECTION

Prevent frozen pipes in cold climates with these precautions:
■ Run hot and cold water lines within insulated areas.
■ Tuck blanket insulation under drainpipes.
■ Wrap heat tape around and insulate water supply pipes that can't be run in an insulated area.
■ Allow for expansion (assume 6 inches for every 50 feet of pipe) if you use plastic pipe.
■ Install a freeze-proof outside hose bibcock. Or, you can install a drain-and-waste valve inside the house in the line to the bibcock to shut it off and drain it for the winter.

GAS LINES

Homeowners are not permitted to install gas lines. If you are relocating or installing a gas range, cooktop, clothes dryer, or water heater that requires moving or installing gas lines, hire a gas-certified plumber. The installer will secure the necessary permit and pressure-test the lines.

Extending a line to move an appliance might require a larger pipe if the run is very long. Adding a gas range or cooktop might require a larger main gas supply pipe for the house to meet the increased demand.

DISHWASHER SHUTOFF VALVES

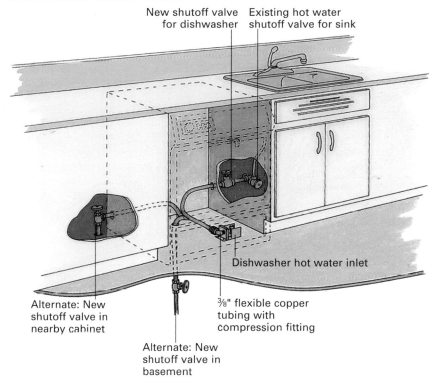

New shutoff valve for dishwasher

Existing hot water shutoff valve for sink

Dishwasher hot water inlet

Alternate: New shutoff valve in nearby cabinet

⅜" flexible copper tubing with compression fitting

Alternate: New shutoff valve in basement

SINK AND REFRIGERATOR SHUTOFFS

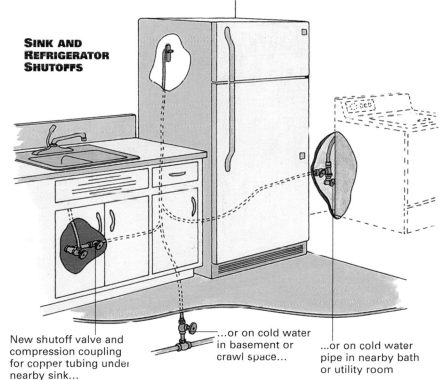

New shutoff valve and compression coupling for copper tubing under nearby sink...

...or on cold water in basement or crawl space...

...or on cold water pipe in nearby bath or utility room

RANGE HOODS

Mechanical ventilation removes cooking odors and excess water vapor from the kitchen.

A range vent system should be rated to move 200 to 400 cubic feet of air per minute (CFM) for average kitchens, more for large kitchens. The hood must be at least 30 inches above the cooking surface.

Plan the duct for the shortest possible run and the fewest turns. The maximum allowable length is usually 25 feet, with turns totaling no more than 180 degrees. The duct must terminate outside the house with an approved roof or wall cap, not in an attic, crawl space, or basement. A backdraft damper is required to prevent outside air from flowing back in.

Both round and rectangular duct sections are available at home centers and large hardware stores. Route round duct through free space, such as attics and crawl spaces; run rectangular ductwork inside walls. The installation instructions for the hood will specify the minimum duct size (usually 7 or 8 inches in diameter for round ducts, 3¼×10 inches for rectangular ducts). Transition sections connect the duct to the fan unit or join round duct to rectangular duct. If you can't find what you need, a sheet metal shop can fabricate it.

Install the duct before insulating the walls. Extend the duct far enough through the wall or ceiling so the remaining pieces can be connected when the cabinets and hood are installed. Secure each joint with a sheet-metal screw and seal it with duct tape.

The illustrations at left show a variety of range venting options. Although building codes provide range hood specifications, the codes don't require one. So a popular option, not shown, is the ductless range hood, which recirculates air through a filter that traps smoke and grease.

RANGE VENTING OPTIONS

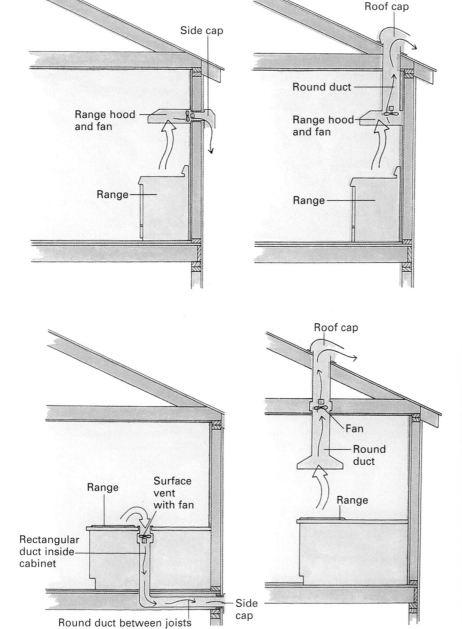

Side cap

Range hood and fan

Range

Roof cap

Round duct

Range hood and fan

Range

Range

Surface vent with fan

Rectangular duct inside cabinet

Round duct between joists

Side cap

Roof cap

Fan

Round duct

Range

RANGE HOOD CODE

CLEARANCE
■ 30 inches of clear space is required above the range top
■ vent outlet must be at least 3 feet from a building opening or the property line

DUCT
■ must be made of 26-gauge metal or heavier
■ must have a smooth interior
■ must be fitted with a backdraft damper to prevent cold outside air from entering the building

INSTALLING WALL AND BASE CABINETS

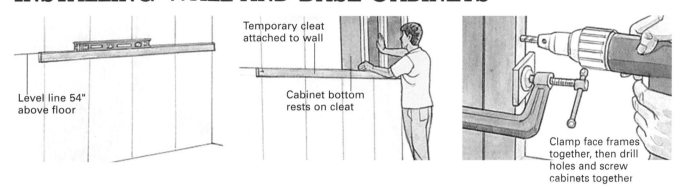

Level line 54" above floor

Temporary cleat attached to wall

Cabinet bottom rests on cleat

Clamp face frames together, then drill holes and screw cabinets together

INSTALLING WALL CABINETS

Have someone help when you install kitchen wall cabinets. They are moderately heavy and you will need both of your hands free to drive in the fasteners. Here's how to do it:

1. Remove the cabinet doors.

2. Find the studs, either from the plan or from the line of drywall screws. Snap chalk lines to indicate the stud centers.

3. Mark the wall 54 inches above the floor at both ends of the planned cabinets—the standard height for wall cabinets. Snap a horizontal chalk line between the marks.

4. Using long drywall screws or double-headed nails, attach a temporary 1×3 cleat to the wall, with its upper edge along the line.

5. With your helper holding the first (usually the corner) cabinet in place on the 1×3, drill pilot holes and drive 2½-inch-long roundhead screws through the cabinet's top hanging strip into the studs. If you installed blocking before the drywall (see page 97), you don't have to hit the studs.

6. Hang the rest of the wall cabinets the same way, butting the cabinet faces together.

7. Clamp the face frames of adjacent cabinets together, keeping the faces flush. Drill through the first frame into the second one at the top, bottom, and middle. Fasten the frames together with 2½-inch drywall screws. Countersink the screws.

8. Drill pilot holes and drive 2½-inch roundhead screws through the cabinet's bottom hanging strip into the wall studs.

9. Remove the 1×3 cleat, then rehang the cabinet doors.

INSTALLING THE BASE CABINETS

Although kitchen base cabinets are heavy, you can install them without help. Here is the general procedure:

1. Remove the cabinet doors and drawers.

2. If you haven't done so already, find and mark the centers of the studs, then snap vertical chalk lines.

3. Using a long level, determine if the floor has a high spot where the cabinets will sit. If there is, mark the spot. Mark the wall 34½ inches above the mark.

4. Using a long level, mark a level line through the mark on the wall. This indicates the tops of the base cabinets.

5. Set the first cabinet in place, and shim it, if necessary, to bring it to the level line. You may have to shim the front and back to level the cabinet both ways.

6. Drill pilot holes and drive drywall screws through the back frame of the cabinet into the wall studs.

7. After each cabinet is fastened at the back, saw or chisel the shims flush with the cabinet.

8. Shim and attach the remaining base cabinets the same way. As you go, make sure the edges of the front faces butt perfectly. If necessary, place shims between the cabinets at the rear to make the fronts butt tightly.

9. One at a time, clamp the face frames of adjacent cabinets together. Drill through the first frame into the next one at the top, bottom, and middle. Fasten the frames together with 2½-inch drywall screws. Countersink the screws.

10. Rehang the cabinet doors.

Level line 34½" above high spot on floor

Stud centerline

Trim shims flush with edge of cabinet

Clamp face frames together, then drill holes and screw cabinets together

BATHS

PLANNING

Although a bathroom is smaller than a kitchen, planning one can take just as much time. One reason is the number and size of waste pipes. The smaller waste pipes (1½- and 2-inch) run through the centers of studs and joists and 3-inch pipes can run between wall studs. But 3-inch pipes with fittings and 4-inch pipes won't fit in a 2×4 wall. You might have to construct a 2×6 wall—a plumbing wall—to conceal the largest pipes.

Further complicating bathroom design is the need to slope drain lines ⅛ to ¼ inch per foot, which can pose problems with ceiling heights on the floor below.

Before you get any permits or begin construction, study your plans carefully and verify all details and specifications with a plumber and building officials.

THE CODE

Study the code requirements below, and make sure your design conforms to them. If it is impossible to do so, ask your code official if there is a way to solve the problem without changing the locations of your fixtures. Many plumbing inspectors are former plumbers and are used to solving such problems.

EXISTING PLUMBING

Determine how the new plumbing will tie in with the existing system. You need to know how and where the 3- or 4-inch drain and waste line will pass through the foundation wall and at what height it will have to run in order to maintain the ⅛- to ¼-inch-per-foot slope to its connection with the existing line.

WATER HEATER

Check the size and location of your water heater. If it is too small to support an additional bathroom, you can install a larger heater or place a second unit closer to the new bathroom.

FIXTURES

Verify the sizes and locations of plumbing fixtures, and check the manufacturer's rough-in dimensions. This is critical for bathtubs and prefabricated shower units. Be sure the drain location is specified for bathtubs (either right-hand or left-hand), and make sure the drain falls between two joists, not on a joist. If it does fall on a joist, cut out part of the joist and frame around the drain with headers before you install the fixture.

FRAMING DETAILS

Double-check the bathroom framing details. You might need to add blocking for tubs, built-in shower stalls, wall-hung toilets and lavatories, and grab rails. Also, decide whether accessories such as towel racks, toilet tissue holders, medicine cabinets, and soap dishes require blocking, wall recesses, or other framing modifications.

Plan the locations for plumbing access panels for tubs, showers, and spas. The panels can affect the finish decor.

CODE REQUIREMENTS

WATER CLOSETS (TOILETS)
Water closets cannot use more than 1.6 gallons per flush. Clear space around a toilet must extend at least
■ 15 inches from center to a wall
■ 12 inches from center to a tub
■ 21 inches in front

SHOWERS
A showerhead can flow 2.5 gallons per minute (gpm) or less at 80 pounds per square inch (psi).

Water temperature cannot exceed 120 degrees F. The shower control valve must be of the thermostatic or pressure balance type. The floor of a shower must have an area of at least 900 square inches that contains a circle at least 30 inches in diameter.

TRAPS
A clothes washer or laundry tub cannot discharge into a trap serving the kitchen sink. Every fixture must have its own trap, except these:
■ one with an integral trap (such as a toilet)
■ multibowl sinks and up to three individual lavatories with outlets no more than 30 inches apart

CLEANOUTS
Provide drain cleanouts
■ when direction changes more than 45 degrees
■ every 40 feet regardless of the number of turns
Cleanouts must have front access of at least

12 inches for pipes up to 3 inches in diameter or 18 inches for pipes over 3 inches in diameter.

VENT TERMINALS
Vents must not terminate
■ under windows or doors
■ within 5 horizontal feet of doors or windows 2 feet or less above the opening
Roof vents must terminate
■ at least 6 inches above the high side of the roof where it passes through
■ at least 1 foot from a vertical surface

BACKING REQUIREMENTS

If your plans don't specify special backing board instead of ordinary drywall for tiled areas and other water-resistant surfaces, consult a tile setter about requirements.

DELIVERY OF LARGE ITEMS

Make sure your bathroom doorway is wide enough for delivery of a prefabricated shower or bathtub. If not, either leave part of a wall unfinished until after the items have been delivered or move the unit into the bathroom before framing the room.

ACCESS CONSIDERATIONS

Most falls involving elderly persons take place in bathrooms. For additional safety, incorporate grab rails into your design. The dimensions and features below are taken from the Americans with Disabilities Act, 28 CFR, Part 36, Appendix A, for wheelchair access. They work well for general safety protection, too. Build as many of these features into your bathroom design as you can.

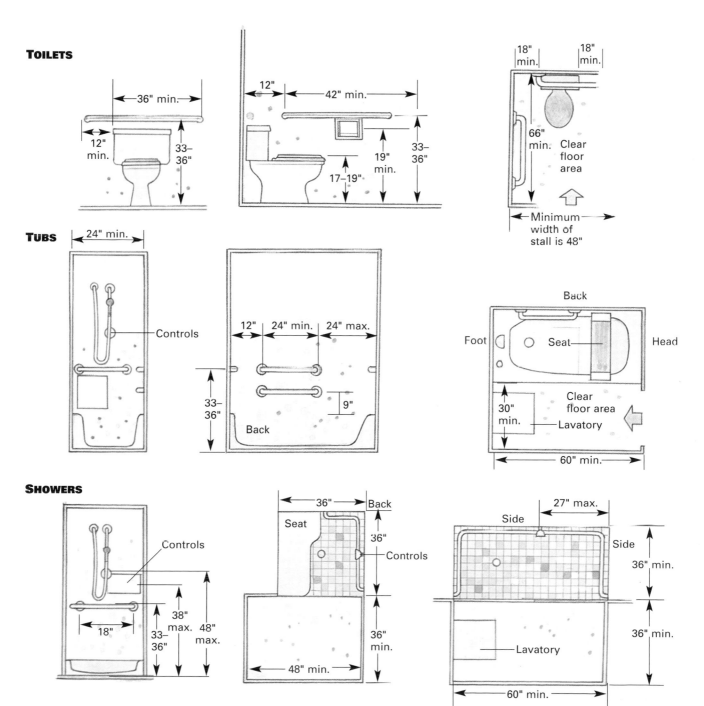

TOILETS

TUBS

SHOWERS

BATHROOM PLANS

SIZE

Many people skimp on space in bathroom planning. No other room in the house will benefit more from a couple of extra feet in both directions. Make your bath spacious, not cramped.

The floor plans on these pages show some possible arrangements of standard fixtures in rooms of different sizes. Deluxe features such as spas require additional space.

LOCATION

A bathroom's location should be determined by who uses it and how frequently:
■ guests—locate bathroom near social spaces (living and dining rooms)
■ homeowner—make bathroom accessible only from master bedroom
■ other family members—place bathroom close to bedrooms

TYPICAL FULL-BATH LAYOUTS

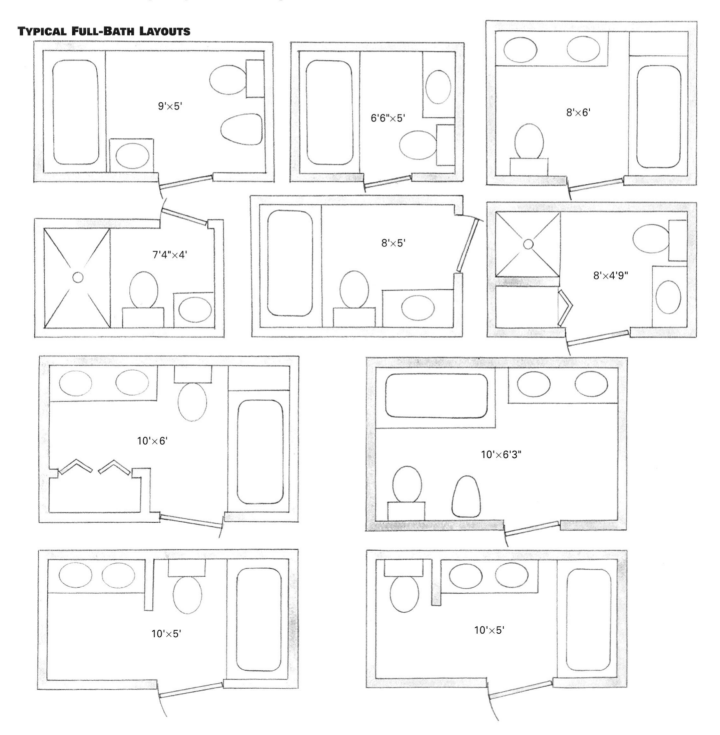

TYPICAL HALF-BATH LAYOUTS

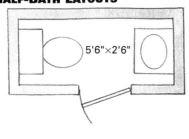

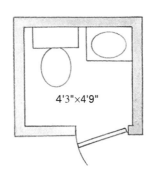

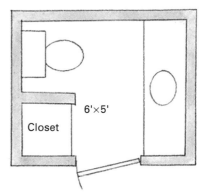

TYPICAL MULTIUSER-BATH LAYOUTS

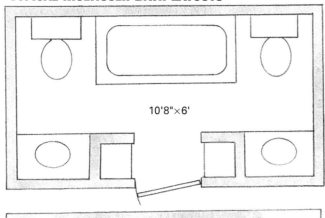

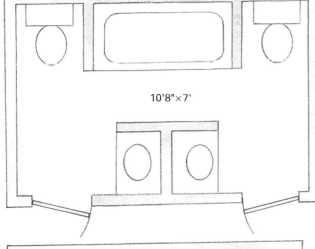

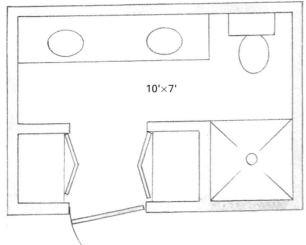

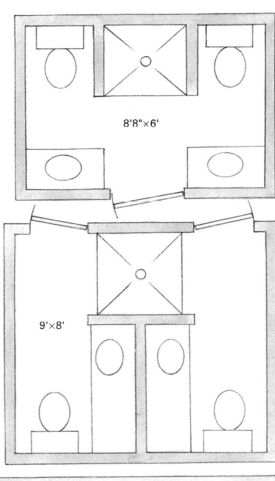

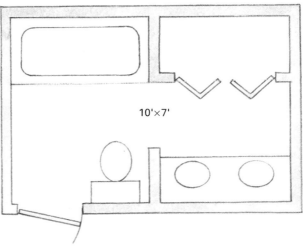

BATHROOM FRAMING

PLUMBING WALL

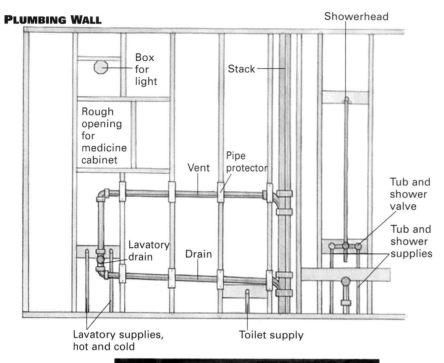

ROUGH FRAMING

Frame the bathroom floor, walls, and ceiling with basic rough carpentry techniques: studs 16 inches on-center, double top plates, and headers over doors and windows. Some framing details are unique to bathrooms, however. Most differences involve plumbing, so consult a plumber early in the framing work to learn about special needs. Details to consider include the following:

FRAMING FOR BATHROOM FIXTURES

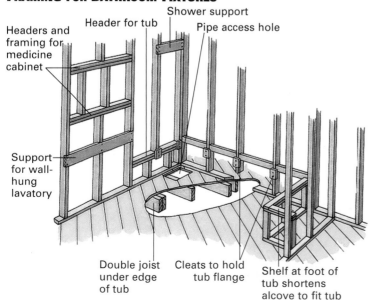

BATHTUBS AND TOILETS

Bathtubs, particularly large luxury tubs or cast iron tubs, can be very heavy. The tub should be located over or near a foundation wall, girder, or bearing wall. If it is not, the joists will probably be strong enough to support a tub placed perpendicular to them if they are properly sized, are not weakened by notches or holes, and are supported solidly at the ends on the foundation or girders.

If the tub lies parallel to the floor joists or is perpendicular to them but centered over a long span, double the joists under the tub.

A toilet may require special floor framing to provide enough room for the large closet bend. If a joist is in the way, cut the joist and support it with a header. Double the header and joists that support it if you have to cut more than one joist.

PLUMBING WALLS

Large 3- and 4-inch-diameter drain and vent pipes are usually concealed inside a wall that's called a plumbing wall. It is convenient to group all or most of the fixtures along a single plumbing wall, as shown in the illustration at left, so a single drain can serve all of them.

Some pipes—such as a 4-inch soil stack, a 3-inch stack with fittings, or even a large shower valve—will not fit inside a 2×4 wall. You could probably fir out the wall where necessary by nailing 2×2s to the studs, but it is simpler and better to frame the entire wall with 2×6 or 2×8 plates and studs.

WING WALLS

Short walls that enclose the end of a tub, shower, or similar area should be framed like ordinary partition walls if they extend to the ceiling. Such walls often end just below ceiling height to create an open feeling, however, so they have no support along the top and one edge. These walls—wing walls, as shown on page 95—must be stabilized.

One way to make a short wing wall sturdy is to butt it against and attach it to a rigid construction, such as a vanity, a built-in tub, or built-in linen shelves. Another way is to sheath the wall on both sides with plywood, fastened with drywall screws, before applying the final finish of backerboard or drywall.

INSTALLING PREFABRICATED TUB OR SHOWER UNIT

Length of enclosure specified by manufacturer

Nailing flange

Studs spaced for faucet assembly

PREFABRICATED UNITS

A prefabricated bathtub or shower unit is usually supported by framing around three sides. Build the walls using standard stud framing techniques. Adjust the stud spacings where the tub and shower controls will be installed so that a stud will not be in the way.

The length of the enclosure for the unit must be accurate, so check the manufacturer's instructions for dimensions, or measure the unit itself at its base.

If the enclosure walls stop short of the ceiling, they are wing walls. Construct them as explained on the previous page.

The drain in a shower base is difficult to tighten after the shower unit is installed, which makes it prone to leakage. Make sure you follow the base manufacturer's instructions exactly, and install and tighten the drain before setting the unit in place.

Frame in an access panel on the back of the wall where the shower valve or tub faucet will be. This will allow you to get to the plumbing for maintenance and repair.

SUNKEN TUBS

A sunken tub requires support from below. This support could be a concrete slab on the ground for a bathroom over a crawl space. Or, it could be dropped floor joists supported by walls for bathrooms over a basement or a first floor.

Place a fiberglass tub on a ½-inch layer of mortar or quick-setting plaster to provide maximum support. Foam is often used to support fiberglass tubs to prevent cracking. After setting the tub into the bedding, don't step into the tub until the material has set; deflection of the tub bottom into it will make a permanent gap between the tub and the support.

Place fiberglass insulation around the tub before closing in the walls to retain heat.

SUNKEN TUB OVER SHALLOW CRAWL SPACE

Subfloor

Tile

Plywood

Short stud wall

1×6 cleat

Joist

Tub

Crawl space

Double header

Insulation

Concrete pad

½" grout

Foundation and framing

BATHROOM PLUMBING

DRAIN, WASTE, AND VENT

Because of the toilet, a bathroom always requires a 3-inch drain. Plumbing restraints complicate the job of running a pipe from the new bathroom to the main drain. That's because the drainpipe must have a consistent slope of 1/8 to 1/4 inch per foot and there may be a limited number of places where a new pipe can connect to the old. Codes restrict which fittings can be used to join branch and main drain; usually a Y, a combination, or a similar long-sweep fitting is required to ensure proper flow. A tee and cleanout are usually installed where the old and new systems meet.

Even when all of these conditions are satisfied, obstacles such as heating ducts or structural members might have to be moved. You might even have to change the proposed pipe routing.

All fixtures must be vented to the roof. If clustered near each other, they can share a common vent, which must be a minimum of 2 inches in diameter. Distance between fixtures is limited by the code-specified trap-arm distance—the maximum distance between the outlet of a trap and its vent pipe. The distance depends on the size of the drain pipe; it is commonly 3½ feet for 1½-inch pipe, and 6 feet for 2-inch pipe.

When connecting a horizontal vent to the roof vent, change direction in the attic rather than below the wall plates to avoid boring holes through too many wall studs.

Changes in vent pipe direction from vertical to horizontal must be made at least 6 inches above the flood line of the fixture (approximately 24 inches above the floor for a bathtub, 40 inches for a sink).

Inspection of completed rough plumbing includes a test for leaks. For this test, all stub-outs are sealed with temporary plugs. To keep water in the new pipes from flowing into the existing plumbing system, plumbers usually insert an inflatable test plug into the cleanout tee where the systems meet to hold water back. To make the test, the pipes, including vent pipes, are filled with water to a specified height above the drain (usually 10 feet).

SUPPLY PIPES

Because they are smaller and not restricted in slope or length, the water supply pipes are always installed after the drain and vent pipes. If you connect new copper pipes to existing galvanized pipes, use a special dielectric union or intermediate brass fitting to minimize corrosion caused by joining different metals that are constantly exposed to water.

Supply pipes are normally tested by capping all stub-outs and pumping air into the pipes to a specified pressure. If you connect new pipes to existing pipes, water pressure from the house system will be sufficient for a leak test.

ROUGH-IN DIMENSIONS

Every fixture has recommended rough-in dimensions for drain and water supply stubs. They are fairly standard for most fixtures, but check the manufacturer's specifications for special items such as luxury bathtubs, elongated toilets, or pedestal sinks. Also, be sure to verify whether the dimensions are from the finish floor or subfloor.

TYPICAL FIXTURE ROUGH-IN DIMENSIONS

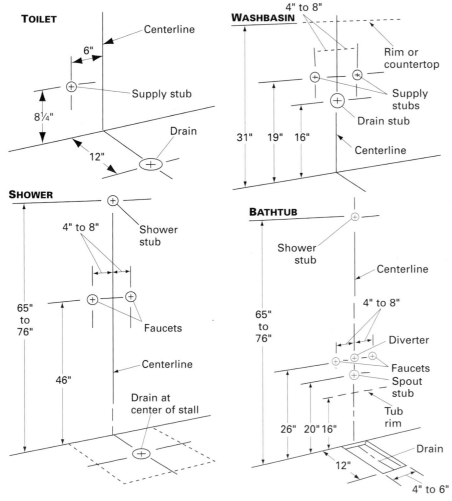

HEATING

A bathroom addition can be heated by extending the existing forced-air or hot-water heating system, adding an electric baseboard or wall heater, or by installing a direct-vent gas heater.

Bathrooms have limited wall space, so it might be difficult to find a good location for a forced-air register. You can usually put one under the toe-kick of the vanity cabinet by bringing a duct up through the floor. Use a transition elbow to connect the register to a ¾-inch by 10-inch rectangular duct that fits horizontally under the cabinet. Cut a hole into the toe-kick for the duct, set the vanity in place, and install the register grill.

A bathroom usually requires no more than 4 feet of hydronic baseboard heating. If you need more, install a compact, fan-forced convection unit under the vanity.

Electric wall heaters can be wired to a 120- or 240-volt circuit. The 240-volt circuit requires three-wire cable and a double circuit breaker. The heating unit might have an integral thermostat or might require a separate thermostat on the bathroom wall.

A direct-vent gas wall heater puts out a lot of heat and is inexpensive to install because it requires no chimney.

VENTILATION

A bathroom without a window that can be opened must have an exhaust fan. It's a good idea to install one in any bathroom to force moisture and odors to the outside.

A bathroom fan should be ducted to the outside through the roof or a wall. To install a bathroom fan, set its housing between a pair of ceiling joists. Cut a 4½-inch-diameter hole through the roof or wall, and install a termination cap. Run 4-inch flexible duct from the fan housing to the cap.

Run a two-wire, 12-gauge feeder cable from the circuit breaker panel to the fan junction box. Then run cable from the fan to a switch box on the wall, using two-wire, three-wire, or a pair of two-wire cables, depending on the number of fan features that need switches. All wires in this switch loop will be hot, so mark any white wires with black tape or paint.

WALLS AND CEILING

After the plumbing, wiring, duct work, and framing are inspected, install insulation and cover the walls and ceilings.

Install insulation, then install polyethylene sheeting over the insulation and framing as a vapor barrier, stapling it to studs and joists. Cut it out around electrical boxes and plumbing stub-outs.

You can apply two coats of latex vapor-barrier paint instead of plastic sheeting. You will probably have to special-order the paint from a wholesaler, though, because retail paint stores rarely stock it. (Glidden Insul-Aid is one brand.) Apply a wall or ceiling finish over the vapor-barrier paint as you would any latex primer.

Windowsills above a tub or shower are likely to get wet from a showerhead, so wrap the rough sill with plastic to prevent the water from reaching and rotting the framing.

To minimize sound transmission from the bathroom, install insulation in the interior as well as the exterior walls. For maximum sound deadening, frame the interior walls with double studs or apply a double layer of wallboard. Some builders install solid-core doors to deaden sound.

Use water-resistant wallboard or special tile backerboard in wet areas, such as shower walls or around the bathtub. Use fiberglass mesh tape and moisture-resistant joint compound to seal the joints. You also can use Type I tile mastic to seal the joints of the cement backerboard.

Paint the walls and ceiling with alkyd (oil-base) rather than latex paints—except the vapor-barrier paint. Although special vinyl paints are often recommended for sealing fresh wallboard, use a durable alkyd primer to create sufficient tooth for oil-base finish paint. To save time and effort, paint the walls and ceiling before you install the cabinets and fixtures.

FLOORING

Installation of the floor covering must be coordinated with installation of bathtub, toilet, vanity, and any other fixtures that sit on the floor. Flooring can be cut and fitted around fixtures, but it is easier and better to install it (except carpeting) before setting fixtures. Putting down the finish floor first helps keep water from getting between the floor and subfloor. It also eliminates the gaps in the flooring and the necessity to caulk around the fixtures.

If the finish flooring requires underlayment (as do resilient materials or tile), install underlayment-grade hardboard or plywood instead of particleboard. Particleboard expands and deteriorates more rapidly than other materials if moisture seeps through to it.

Install ceramic floor tile over a mortar bed or stable plywood (½-inch CC-plugged is recommended over the subfloor). Use epoxy-base adhesive to lay the tile.

INDEX

METRIC CONVERSIONS

U.S. Units to Metric Equivalents			Metric Units to U.S. Equivalents		
To Convert From	Multiply By	To Get	To Convert From	Multiply By	To Get
Inches	25.4	Millimeters	Millimeters	0.0394	Inches
Inches	2.54	Centimeters	Centimeters	0.3937	Inches
Feet	30.48	Centimeters	Centimeters	0.0328	Feet
Feet	0.3048	Meters	Meters	3.2808	Feet
Yards	0.9144	Meters	Meters	1.0936	Yards
Square inches	6.4516	Square centimeters	Square centimeters	0.1550	Square inches
Square feet	0.0929	Square meters	Square meters	10.764	Square feet
Square yards	0.8361	Square meters	Square meters	1.1960	Square yards
Acres	0.4047	Hectares	Hectares	2.4711	Acres
Cubic inches	16.387	Cubic centimeters	Cubic centimeters	0.0610	Cubic inches
Cubic feet	0.0283	Cubic meters	Cubic meters	35.315	Cubic feet
Cubic feet	28.316	Liters	Liters	0.0353	Cubic feet
Cubic yards	0.7646	Cubic meters	Cubic meters	1.308	Cubic yards
Cubic yards	764.55	Liters	Liters	0.0013	Cubic yards

To convert from degrees Fahrenheit (F) to degrees Celsius (C), first subtract 32, then multiply by $\frac{5}{9}$.

To convert from degrees Celsius to degrees Fahrenheit, multiply by $\frac{9}{5}$, then add 32.